MW01146550

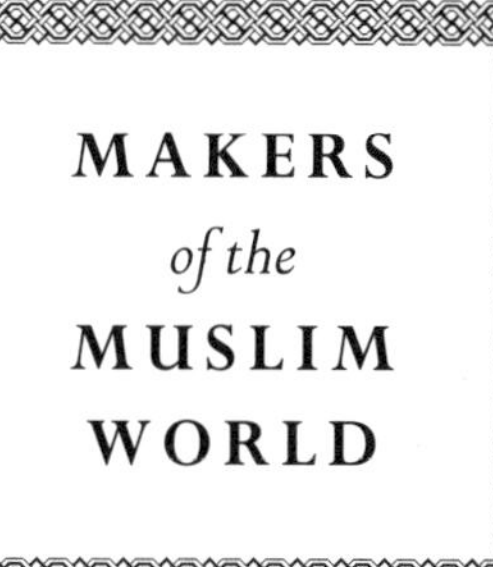

Hasan al-Banna

SELECTION OF TITLES IN THE MAKERS OF THE MUSLIM WORLD SERIES

Series editor: Patricia Crone,
Institute for Advanced Study, Princeton

Abd al-Ghani al-Nabulusi, Samer Akkach
'Abd al-Malik, Chase F. Robinson
Abd al-Rahman III, Maribel Fierro
Abu Nuwas, Philip Kennedy
Ahmad al-Mansur, Mercedes García-Arenal
Ahmad ibn Hanbal, Christopher Melchert
Ahmad Riza Khan Barelwi, Usha Sanyal
Akbar, André Wink
Al-Ma'mun, Michael Cooperson
Al-Mutanabbi, Margaret Larkin
Amir Khusraw, Sunil Sharma
Ashraf 'Ali Thanawi, Muhammad Qasim Zaman
Chinggis Khan, Michal Biran
El Hajj Beshir Agha, Jane Hathaway
Fazlallah Astarabadi and the Hurufis, Shazad Bashir
Ghazali, Eric Ormsby
Husain Ahmad Madani, Barbara Metcalf
Ibn 'Arabi, William C. Chittick
Ibn Fudi, Ahmad Dallal
Ikhwan al-Safa, Godefroid de Callatay
Karim Khan Zand, John R. Perry
Mehmed Ali, Khaled Fahmy
Mu'awiya ibn abi Sufyan, R. Stephen Humphreys
Nasser, Joel Gordon
Sa'di, Homa Katouzian
Shaykh Mufid, Tamima Bayhom-Daou
Usama ibn Munqidh, Paul M. Cobb

For current information and details of other books in the series, please visit www.oneworld-publications.com

Hasan al-Banna

GUDRUN KRÄMER

ONEWORLD
OXFORD

HASAN AL-BANNA

Published by Oneworld Publications 2010

A CIP record for this title is available
from the British Library

ISBN 978–1–85168–430–4

Typeset by Jayvee, Trivandrum, India
Printed and bound in India for Imprint Digital

Oneworld Publications
UK: 185 Banbury Road, Oxford, OX2 7AR, England
USA: 38 Greene Street, 4th Floor, New York, NY 10013, USA
www.oneworld-publications.com

CONTENTS

INTRODUCTION

Hasan al-Banna (1906–49) was the founder and lifelong leader of the Egyptian Muslim Brotherhood, the largest and most influential Islamic movement in the Arab Middle East, formed in 1928 and still active in Egypt and other Muslim countries from Jordan and Yemen to Nigeria and Indonesia. Until Sayyid Qutb (1906–66), who only joined the Muslim Brotherhood after al-Banna's death, emerged, posthumously, as a powerful voice of modern Islamism, Hasan al-Banna embodied the Brotherhood as no other individual did. Even today, he continues to evoke strong feelings as reflected in a rich and varied literature, ranging from hagiography to angry polemic. Yet no scholarly biography has so far been published in either Arabic or any other relevant language. This may be due to the problematic nature of the sources as much as to the sensitivity of the subject – that is, Islamism past and present. Not that there is a dearth of writings on the subject. The most widely read focus on a limited number of issues: Islam and power, Islam and gender and, of course, Islam, *jihad* and martyrdom. These issues are of obvious relevance to the present study, but they do not constitute its prime concerns. At the centre stands al-Banna's project of establishing a moral order based on what he conceived of as "true Islam."

Hasan al-Banna's life and thought are so closely intertwined with the movement he founded and inspired that it is difficult to distinguish the private man from the public figure. For this reason, this study deals as much with the Muslim Brothers as with Hasan al-Banna himself, attempting to put them firmly in context. This sounds perhaps more trivial than it is. There is a tendency to treat Islamism as a subject located on a planet called Islam, different from all other socio-political and cultural phenomena. The "Islamic exceptionalism" resulting from this approach tends to underrate the commonalities of thought, idiom and practice between Islamists on the one hand and their "secular" contemporaries on the other. As a historian, one ought to try to counter this tendency.

Some technical remarks are called for. To illustrate al-Banna's thought, or discourse, I have quoted amply from his writings, notably his *Memoirs*, tracts and talks published in the Muslim Brothers' press. Unfortunately, these texts have been repeatedly reissued, sometimes without indicating the publisher and the year of publication. A number of al-Banna's tracts are available in English translation. Whenever possible, I have referred to Charles Wendell's *Five Tracts of Hasan Al-Banna'* in addition to the original Arabic, taken from the collection of tracts *Majmu'at rasa'il*, of which there exist several editions with different selections. My own translations are occasionally based on Wendell's but depart from his whenever this seemed necessary. Footnotes are always a touchy subject: instructions for the *Makers of the Muslim World* series ask authors not to use any footnotes at all. Given the controversial nature of much of the material, I felt this was impossible. Some compromise had to be found. In the end, I decided to provide footnotes for statements, such as membership figures or the role of women in the Muslim Brotherhood, that I thought might be of interest to a wider readership or elicit debate. The main body of the narrative relies on what passes as Hasan al-Banna's *Memoirs* (*Mudhakkirat al-da'wa wa-l-da'iya*), the *Letters* edited by his brother Jamal, as well as a number of studies on the Muslim Brotherhood, notably R. Mitchell and Lia on the one hand, and 'Abd al-Halim, Ahmad, Mahmud, Sha'ir, al-Sisi and Zaki on the other. Transliteration has been simplified so as to make the text readable while allowing the specialist to identify names, terms and titles. Al-Banna is written without the final hamza, which according to the rules of Arabic grammar it requires. However, the al-Banna family consistently spells its name without the hamza, and even as an orientalist, I saw no need to be as it were holier than the Pope, if this is a proper expression to use in the present context.

FAMILY BACKGROUND, EDUCATION AND EARLY CAREER

RURAL PIETY

From an early age, Hasan al-Banna was influenced by (Arab) reform Islam of the Salafi type, popular Sufism of the "sober" kind, and Egyptian patriotism, as understood and lived in the socio-cultural milieu he was raised in. It is with this milieu, or, to be more precise, with his family that the story must begin. Hasan al-Banna's father, Ahmad b. 'Abd al-Rahman b. Muhammad, was in fact a remarkable man who would deserve a study of his own, to explore more deeply the lives and concerns of educated people in the Egyptian countryside at the turn of the twentieth century.

Hasan al-Banna's father was born in 1300/1882 into a family of small landowners in the village of Shimshira on the westernmost branch of the Nile, not far from where it flows into the Mediterranean at Rosetta. Administratively, Simshira was located in the district of Fuwwa, which was then part of al-Gharbiyya province. His mother came from a family of "knowledge and religion"; her brother was a *faqih*, a Qur'an reciter, in the neighbouring village of Sindiyun. Hasan al-Banna's younger brother Jamal relates that when his grandmother was pregnant with her second child, she had a dream that her son would be called Ahmad and would learn the Qur'an by heart. The dream came true: Ahmad entered a *kuttab* or

Qur'anic school – the only type of school then available in a small Egyptian village – at the age of four and acquired a lifelong love of learning.

Ahmad was born the year the British occupied Egypt. This was the beginning of the era of Lord Cromer (Sir Evelyn Baring), who as British agent and consul-general effectively governed the country from 1883 to 1907. Like many members of the English ruling class, Cromer did not believe in advanced public education, least of all for the peasant population. In his view, rural men and women, if they were to have any education at all, should be given a practical training designed to make them, as a British official in neighbouring Palestine was later to put it, "useful and content." This applied to Britain as much as to the colonies, but especially to the latter. Government schools of the European type were liable to manufacture nationalist "demagogues" and "malcontents," who would not be satisfied with their station in life.[1] Many members of the Egyptian upper class shared his views. Schools also cost money. For these reasons, government investment in rural education was limited, and literacy rates remained very low. Take Shimshira: in 1907, the Egyptian census registered 192 inhabited houses in Shimshira with a total 1,226 residents, of whom a mere thirteen, all of them men, were able to read and write – a notoriously vague category which could mean anything from being able to scribble one's name to easy fluency in literary Arabic. (One should also bear in mind that some people were able to read without being able to write.)

Ahmad al-Banna did not wish to join his elder brother in cultivating their land as this would not leave him sufficient time to pursue knowledge. Instead, he resolved to learn the craft of repairing watches, an unusual choice for a village boy of his time and age. Supported by his parents, who both held religious learning in high esteem, Ahmad went to Alexandria to train as an apprentice with a well-known master of the craft. At the same time he continued his religious education at the Ibrahim Pasha Mosque, one of the largest mosque colleges, or *madrasa*s, in the country. While al-Azhar was certainly the most widely known institution of higher religious learning in nineteenth-century Egypt, it was not the only one. Muhammad Ali (r. 1805–48) had weakened their position by confiscating their endowments (*awqaf*), yet there still remained several mosque colleges that also trained religious scholars, *'ulama'*, and whose graduates could also serve in various official or semi-official functions, such as *faqih* (legal expert, but in contemporary rural Egypt usually a Qur'an reciter and *kuttab* teacher), *imam* (prayer leader), *khatib* (Friday preacher) or *ma'dhun* (notary for marriages and divorces). The largest and most prestigious was the *madrasa* attached to the al-Ahmadi Mosque in Tanta, which in around 1900 had sixty-eight scholars–teachers or "professors" and 4,173 students, followed by Ibrahim Pasha with forty-three professors and 773 students. For comparison, al-Azhar numbered 250 professors and 10,403 students.[2] It was only at the turn of the century that the provincial *madrasa*s were integrated into the Azhar school system, under the name of "religious institutes."

Upon completing his training, Shaykh Ahmad, as he was now addressed, returned to Shimshira. Though he was not an Azharite, as sometimes claimed in the literature, he still derived prestige, or cultural capital to use Pierre Bourdieu's term, from attending a renowned institution of higher religious learning. For a living, he practised his craft and was therefore known as "al-Sa'ati," the "watchmaker," until he gave it up in the 1940s and used only "al-Banna" for what counted as a family name. At the age of nineteen, Shaykh Ahmad passed the Qur'an examination to be exempted from military service, which he – like most Egyptians – dreaded. In 1904 he married the younger daughter of a local merchant of dyed and embroidered fabrics, who reportedly had a little more money than his father's family. The bride, Umm al-Sa'd, was only fifteen at the time and rather pretty, of slight build and light complexion (always highly appreciated as a sign of distinction), who unlike the peasant girls had never had to toil in the fields. She was also intelligent, alert and strong-willed, if not obstinate, qualities her eldest son Hasan inherited, along with her facial features and moderate height.

Shortly after, Shaykh Ahmad left Shimshira to settle in al-Mahmudiyya, situated a little to the south on the other bank of the

Nile, from where the Mahmudiyya Canal started, dug during the reign of Muhammad 'Ali to carry Nile water to Alexandria and named after the Ottoman sultan Mahmud II. Al-Mahmudiyya was close to the al-'Atf pumping station and for this reason the place names al-'Atf and al-Mahmudiyya were often used interchangeably. Like many other places in the Egyptian countryside, where rural and urban settlements shared basic traits, al-Mahmudiyya could be characterized as either a large village or a small town, with little difference between the two. Semi-urban might be the best term to describe it. It was larger than Shimshira and definitely more lively. With regard to the general level of education, however, the two were quite similar: in 1907, al-Mahmudiyya had about 1,000 houses with just over 6,000 inhabitants, of whom 375 were able to read and write; the relevant figures for al-'Atf were some 250 houses, 1,500 inhabitants and sixty-six literate individuals; in both places, not a single woman was registered as being able to read and write. Still, al-Mahmudiyya had a social and cultural life of its own that was geared to the tastes of local landowners and merchants. Theatre and music troupes touring the country came to both al-'Atf and al-Mahmudiyya; a trade union was active among the workers of the pumping station, and so these were not places untouched by modern life.

In al-Mahmudiyya, Shaykh Ahmad bought a small house for himself and his young wife and opened a shop where he not only repaired clocks and watches but also sold gramophones and gramophone records. The latter is remarkable, for the recording business had only just started in Egypt, with the first commercial recordings being made in 1904. Much of the local production recorded Qur'anic recitation, classical Arabic poetry and religious song, especially poems in praise of the Prophet, and for this reason was not considered blameworthy or forbidden (*munkar*) in terms of the religious-cum-moral categories of Islamic law. There was also a close link with Sufism as Sufi chant as well as Qur'anic recitation required a trained voice. Singers thus trained were addressed as shaykh. 'Abduh al-Hamuli (1841–1901) was perhaps the best-known Egyptian representative of this "high style" of Arabic music so appreciated by

Egyptian audiences. In 1910, Umm Kulthum (b. *c.*1904) made her first public appearances; over the course of her long career she would significantly alter the genre. Shaykh Ahmad was attached to Sufism and endowed with an aesthetic sensibility that he passed on to his children, two of whom, 'Abd al-Rahman and 'Abd al-Basit, wrote poetry; the former also played the *rababa*, a traditional string instrument, and the latter the *'ud*, or lute. 'Abd al-Rahman later wrote Islamic plays for the theatre and 'Abd al-Basit composed a number of songs. Their elder brother Hasan was more attracted to the written word.

Shaykh Ahmad was not just literate in a society that was overwhelmingly illiterate. He enjoyed reading, and not only religious material. His son Jamal recalled how his father cut out serialized detective stories published in *al-Ahram* and bound them in leather. In later years he subscribed to *al-Lata'if al-Musawwara*, a popular illustrated weekly published in 1915–41, building on the earlier *al-Lata'if* (1885–95), which had been a Masonic journal. Still later, he added the weekly *al-Amal*, published in 1925–8 by Munira Thabit, one of the first female newspaper editors in Egypt and a known Wafdist.

Even without an academic degree, Shaykh Ahmad was respected for his piety and religious learning among the community. He befriended members of the local elite, including the mayor (*'umda*), shaykhs and merchants, some of whom shared his passion for religious knowledge. He grew especially close to Shaykh Muhammad Zahran, a blind preacher and teacher at one of the local mosques, who, like himself, held no Azhar degree but was deeply committed to religious study. Among other things Shaykh Zahran edited a journal called *al-Is'ad*, which apparently was modelled on the famous *al-Manar* (*The Lighthouse*), the mouthpiece of the Islamic reform movement known as Salafiyya and represented in Egypt by Muhammad 'Abduh (1849–1905) and Muhammad Rashid Rida (1865–1935). Before long Shaykh Ahmad was invited to serve as prayer leader and Friday preacher at a local mosque. The mayor later also asked him to serve as second *ma'dhun*, at the time an important government official who acted mostly as notary for marriages and divorces. Still, his financial situation was not particularly good, especially after his children were born, at regular intervals, altogether five boys and three girls, one of whom died in her infancy. A grocery shop he opened failed and he incurred losses. He then decided to practise the craft of bookbinding, in which, assisted by his wife, he proved more successful.

The phenomenon of rural men (and possibly even women) engaging in religious scholarship for its own sake, without the prospect of making a career out of it, has been little studied, at least with regard to Egypt. Respecting religious learning and even collecting books was not that unusual in the Egyptian countryside. Sayyid Qutb (1906–66), the educator famously turned Islamist, who was born the same year as Hasan al-Banna into a landowning family in Asyut province, is a case in point, as is Yusuf al-Qaradawi, the influential scholar and "media mufti," who was born two decades later, in 1926, into a less affluent rural family in the Delta. But Shaykh Ahmad did not content himself with studying and debating religious topics with local shaykhs and dignitaries. He began to write books of his own.

His first study was a short treatise on the prayer litany (*wazifa*) of the Maghribi Sufi Ahmad Zarruq (d. 899/1493–4), one of the great masters of the Shadhili tradition to which Shaykh Ahmad himself was attached.[3] Shaykh Zarruq was known for his legalistic style and attitude. Even so, members of the brotherhood attributed magical or protective powers to the *wazifa Zarruqiyya*, and Sufism was generally under attack from reformist circles. Shaykh Ahmad made it his aim to prove that Zarruq's prayer litany was almost entirely based on Qur'anic verses and authentic Hadiths, and thus perfectly "orthodox." The study was first printed in 1330/1912 at his expense; by the 1950s it had seen several reprints. From the defence of a major Sufi text, Shaykh Ahmad moved to the Prophetic Traditions, testifying to the enduring attraction of Hadith studies among the learned, in his own day as much as later. His work on al-Shafi'i's *Musnad* was eventually published in Cairo in two volumes in 1369/1950. There he also lists two more works on the Hadith collections of Abu Da'ud and Abu Hanifa respectively, which apparently remained unpublished.

His most ambitious project, however, was to classify Ahmad b. Hanbal's collection of Prophetic Traditions, the *Musnad*, of which he acquired a copy in 1921–2, when he was about forty years old. As the title, which refers to Hadiths traceable through a particular chain of authorities, suggests, the *Musnad* was arranged according to these "traditionists" (*muhaddith*, *rawi*), and for this reason was difficult to use. To re-order it according to subject matter was a daunting task in which eminent scholars had failed. Even more ambitiously, Shaykh Ahmad also resolved to write a commentary (*sharh*). The work *al-Fath al-rabbani fi tartib musnad al-imam Ahmad b. Hanbal al-Shaybani*, with a commentary entitled *Bulugh al-amani min asrar al-Fath al-rabbani*, was to occupy him for the rest of his life. At the time of his death, in 1958, twenty-two volumes of what was to be a total of twenty-four volumes of *al-Fath al-rabbani* had been printed and were available in various editions, leather bound and on expensive white or less expensive "yellow" paper. The remaining two volumes were completed with the help of his family; the commentary was left unfinished.

Shaykh Ahmad did not see much of the world – apart from a pilgrimage to Mecca he made in the mid-1940s, he never travelled beyond Cairo and the Suez Canal Zone. Yet his intellectual horizon, or "space," was much broader and largely defined by the fields he embraced – Qur'an, Hadith, the life of the Prophet, and Islamic jurisprudence, *fiqh*, combined with Sufi thought and practice of the more sober type – and the language he spoke and indeed mastered, Arabic. In spite of his focus on Ahmad b. Hanbal's *Musnad*, there was no specifically Hanbali or Hanbali Wahhabi bias in the religious upbringing of his children that might explain the choices his son Hasan was later to make. As his work on *al-Fath al-rabbani* progressed, he corresponded with scholars in Egypt and abroad, notably in Syria, Hijaz and Yemen, establishing contacts that were to prove useful to his son in later years.

EARLY EDUCATION

Born in 1906, the first child of a young couple, Hasan al-Banna seems to have had a happy childhood. He was a healthy boy and not afflicted by disease, as many children from poorer families were. The family lived modestly, and it was of course affected by the state of the rural economy, but it was not destitute. Thus they always kept a servant or household help, who was either a member of the family or from the village, and was very much part of the household. Shaykh Ahmad was keen on giving his firstborn an Islamic education but was dissatisfied with the schools to be found locally. It was only in 1915, when Hasan was already nine years old, that Shaykh Ahmad's mentor Muhammad Zahran opened a school that met his expectations. The school in question, Madrasat al-Rashad al-Diniyya, offered more than the ordinary village *kuttab*, for Hasan not only learned parts of the Qur'an and a number of Prophetic Hadiths by heart, but also basic reading and writing as well as some Arabic poetry. In contrast to many others, al-Banna retained fond memories of his early school years and he positively revered his first teacher. In fact his *Memoirs* do not begin with his parents, but with Shaykh Zahran, whose influence derived as much from his learning as from his personality. In an often-quoted passage, Hasan al-Banna commented on the strong emotional and spiritual bond Shaykh Zahran was able to create with his pupils – a bond that was to inspire him for the rest of his life.

When in 1918 Shaykh Zahran left his school, Hasan no longer wanted to stay there. He was now about twelve years old, and his parents hoped that he would continue with his religious education. However, the Azhar school system, which provided an avenue of upward mobility to country boys of modest means, required candidates to have memorized the entire Qur'an – and he had not yet reached this stage. Acting on his own wishes rather than his parents', Hasan opted for the government school in al-Mahmudiyya. In line with British educational policies, instruction focused on religion and practical knowledge that was deemed appropriate for peasants – the three Rs, reading, writing and arithmetic – and these became the focus of his studies. No foreign languages were taught at the school, making future access to a government secondary school virtually impossible.

At school, a teacher suggested that Hasan and his friends join together to "form" their character and manners – a classic example of moral improvement (*takwin al-akhlaq*) through practical training rather than abstract lesson, and thus in line with both contemporary educational theories and the *amr bil-ma'ruf*, the Qur'anic injunction "to enjoin good and prohibit wrong," which was to play a crucial role in al-Banna's career as an Islamic activist. The members of the association, called Jam'iyyat al-Akhlaq al-Adabiyya, prayed together at the appointed times, causing the *imam* of their mosque some anxiety as he calculated the cost of the water they used for their ablutions and the straw mats they dirtied. Characteristically, fines were imposed for all kinds of misdemeanour. Already then Hasan's days were filled and structured by the rhythm of prayer: before school (to be precise – and Hasan al-Banna is precise, albeit not always correct, about time and money in his *Memoirs* – after morning prayer) he continued to memorize the Qur'an, and after school he trained with his father to repair clocks and watches until evening prayer. There was no idleness in his life, not in his boyhood days and even less in his mature years.

It also appears that he engaged in his first acts of vigilantism while still at school in al-Mahmudiyya. Walking along the river one day, he recounts in his *Memoirs*, he observed that in a spot where women went to draw water, workmen had made a nude wooden figure for (the prow of?) the sailing ship they were building, which was of course forbidden, *munkar*. Hasan immediately informed the local police officer, who in turn commended the young man to the inspector of his school. The latter presented him as a model to his fellow students, enjoining them to follow his example and give good counsel to the people (*nasiha*) and to prohibit wrong, whatever shape it might take. Whether fictitious or not, this is a telling story, depicting Hasan al-Banna in his chosen role of the one who speaks truth in the face of those who by ordinary standards were his elders and betters.

Some friends, including his younger brother 'Abd al-Rahman, were not content with improving their own character but set up an association called Society for the Prevention of the Forbidden (Jam'iyyat Man' al-Muharramat). One should perhaps not read too much into a name chosen by boys in their early teens, but it still merits attention that they opted for the term "preventing" the forbidden rather than merely "prohibiting" it, even though in actual fact they did not resort to force. Rather, they sent strongly worded missives to those among their fellow citizens whom who they felt were transgressing Islamic rules, for instance by neglecting prayer or by eating during the month of Ramadan. Women who were observed beating their faces during funerals or following other pre-Islamic (*jahili*) customs were not approached directly; rather their husbands or legal guardians received a letter of warning. Harmless though these acts of religious zeal may have been, people resented them. About six months after the creation of the association, the owner of a coffeehouse finally caught a messenger bringing a letter reprimanding him for employing a female dancer, and told him off in front of his customers. Chastened, the group decided to use "softer" methods in the future.

It is worth noting what Hasan al-Banna characterizes as forbidden (*muharram*), notably the funerary practices that were well known to derive from pharaonic precedents. He does not, however, refer to what Sayyid Qutb evoked so powerfully in his childhood memoirs: magic and sorcery pervading each and every thing, enthralling him then and haunting him throughout his life. Compared to Qutb's stories of raving saints, roaming ghosts, protective charms and the magic effects of Qur'anic recitation, Hasan al-Banna's realm of the forbidden appears positively tame. There is no sense of the destructive potency of the unknown and the terror attached to it. What Hasan al-Banna fought was the illicit – not the eerie and the unsettling.

ENCOUNTERING SUFISM

In 1919, the governorate replaced the type of school he had attended by a new one, called *ibtida'iyya*. Among other things, the reform abolished the higher grades he was about to enter. Aged thirteen and a half, Hasan al-Banna found himself in a difficult situation, for the two careers the family considered appropriate both required him to have fully memorized the Qur'an. This was true not only of the

Religious Institute (*al-ma'had al-dini*) of Alexandria (formerly Ibrahim Pasha), which would have allowed him later to join al-Azhar University, but also of the elementary teachers' training school at Damanhur, the capital of al-Buhayra province, to which al-Mahmudiyya had become attached. After a personal interview with the headmaster Hasan was admitted to the teachers' college on the promise that he would learn the remaining quarter of the Qur'an as quickly as possible.

In contrast to al-Mahmudiyya with its transitional character between large village and small country town, Damanhur was a real city. It had grown significantly during the cotton boom of the 1860s and 1870s that was tied to the American Civil War and the opening of the Suez Canal in 1869, and again during the decade from 1897 to the economic crash of 1907. Alongside Tanta and al-Mansura, both of which had about 20,000 inhabitants, Damanhur was one of the administrative and commercial centres of the Nile Delta, boasting a number of fine buildings and three annual fairs. Yet we get absolutely no sense of the place from reading al-Banna's *Memoirs* and private letters. The only places mentioned there are the school and religious sites, and the only persons his teachers, friends and Sufi shaykhs.

Even politics does not figure prominently in these writings. When Hasan al-Banna was young, Egypt was a colonial society with a colonial economy, dominated by large landowners, and closely tied to foreign interests. His father was born the year the British occupied the country and Hasan was born in the same year as the infamous Dinshaway Incident that fuelled Egyptian nationalism, when a number of villagers were hanged and others flogged in retaliation for the death of a British officer on a shooting trip in the Delta. The years following the First World War were marked by intense patriotic feeling and activity, and involvement in the national struggle (significantly called *jihad*) was later claimed as an essential element of their career by most political activists. The immediate aftermath of the War, when Hasan al-Banna was still at primary school, saw the popular uprising or revolution led by the national movement of the Wafd; in 1922 Egypt became nominally independent and in 1923 a constitution was passed.

Students were at the forefront of national demonstrations and Hasan al-Banna was no exception. He later recalled the rallies and marches staged in al-Mahmudiyya, the nationalist songs and chants, the entry of British soldiers into town and the civil guard formed by its inhabitants to oppose these soldiers. He spoke of "patriotic duties" to be fulfilled and said that "serving the homeland is a mandatory *jihad*." But he also made it plain that religion remained foremost in his mind. In subsequent years he even burned his substantial collection of nationalist poetry and song. Yet the vibrant tone of Egyptian nationalism, of devotion to a higher cause, survived the auto-da-fé, merging with Islamic sentiment to produce the special blend of twentieth-century Egyptian Arab Islamism.

For Hasan al-Banna, the defining aspect of his youth was not school, and neither was it politics. It was religion in general and Sufism in particular; the personal ties built on that basis lasted almost throughout his life. Al-Banna was an adolescent when he trained to become a schoolteacher and not yet seventeen when he left college. At that time puberty, or the teenage years, was not recognized in Egyptian society as a discrete phase in a young person's development, requiring special caution and care. Life was ruled by a strict moral code based on gender segregation, and religious passion may well have coexisted with, or helped to sublimate, physical desire. The subject is frequently discussed in the relevant literature, including in accounts of Islamist writers who insist that his personal experience gave al-Banna a better understanding of ardent youth in later years.

The impact of school and religion are not always easy to distinguish, though, for religion was lived and taught at school as well as outside it, and apart from his father, the men who influenced him most deeply were his teachers. To begin with, it would be wrong to paint too sharp a contrast between religious and secular education. The three-year course at the teachers' training college put heavy emphasis on the Arabic language and religious (i.e., Islamic) studies, and it relied largely on memorization and recitation – "loading the memory without exercising the mind," as Lord Cromer had remarked (*Modern Egypt*, p. 881). It was teachers, of whom Shaykh

Zahran was the first, who urged al-Banna and his friends along the path of religious study and pious practice, and joined them in their endeavours or discussed their concerns with them. Hasan was deeply affected and retained the lesson that "truth is the daughter of study" (*Memoirs*, p. 28). He may already have shown some leadership qualities as a boy, but he never seems to have acted entirely on his own. In this respect, he differed from his father, who spent much of his time in lonely study. Not only was he surrounded by like-minded friends; his teachers provided him with a stable framework, remaining trusted authorities – road signs, *ma'alim al-tariq*, on which Sayyid Qutb was later to write one of the most influential books of modern Islamism. For Hasan al-Banna, it appears, the path was always clear.

If it makes sense to divide his life into distinct phases – and al-Banna does so in his *Memoirs* – his years at Damanhur, when he studied at a government school to become a government employee, constituted his Sufi phase. In his *Memoirs* he recalls being first attracted to the *dhikr* ceremony performed by members of the Hasafiyya Brotherhood in a mosque in al-Mahmudiyya, where he attended Shaykh Zahran's classes between afternoon and evening prayer, when he was twelve years old. Perhaps not surprising for his age, it was the practice that caught his attention, what he later described as their "organized voices and beautiful chant," not their teachings, which at that time he can hardly have known or understood (*Memoirs*, pp. 19f., 27).

The Hasafiyya was a local offshoot of the large and variegated Shadhiliyya order (*tariqa*), and a young one, one of the many branches that developed in the second half of the nineteenth century, the heyday of organized Sufism in Egypt.[4] Most of them were of local significance only and often quite short-lived, depending on the personality and leadership qualities of their shaykhs. The brotherhood took its name from Shaykh Hasanayn al-Hasafi (1848/9–1910), an Azhar scholar of the Shafi'i school, who had been initiated into a new branch of the Shadhiliyya order by its founder, Muhammad b. Muhammad al-Fasi (d. 1872), one of the many Moroccans residing in Mecca; this new branch was identified as the Fasiyya Makkiyya. In the

1870s Shaykh Hasanayn visited Egypt twice and gained a number of adherents, notably in Cairo and Suez. Like many other Sufis, he was not exclusively attached to the Fasiyya Makkiyya, but also initiated into half a dozen other brotherhoods. Around 1878 he broke with it over the correct form of *dhikr* and set up his own *tariqa*, the Hasafiyya Shadhiliyya, which Hasan al-Banna's father seems to have joined at some point.

Hasan al-Banna befriended some of the young Hasafis in al-Mahmudiyya, among them Ahmad al-Sukkari, who was later to become a leading figure in the Society of the Muslim Brothers. He eagerly studied Zarruq's prayer litany (*wazifa*), on which, it will be remembered, his father had written a study, as well as a hagiography of Shaykh Hasanayn al-Hasafi, which had recently been published in Cairo. The Sufi affiliation also eased the transition from Hasan's native al-Mahmudiyya to Damanhur, providing him with new friends and a strong sense of community. Shaykh Hasanayn was buried in Damanhur and Hasan al-Banna visited his tomb almost daily, attended the weekly meeting (*hadra*) of the brethren and studied with a local shaykh. With his friends he paid frequent visits to the tombs of the saints venerated by the Hasafis, walking as far as al-Disuq, some three hours' distance from Damanhur – no doubt something of a regular outing with attendant excitement, but at the same time a practice that was viewed with distinct reserve by Hanbali scholars and Salafi reformers alike, suggesting that rigid Hanbalism in the image of Muhammad b. ʻAbd al-Wahhab and his followers was not what al-Banna sought and practised.

In Ramadan 1341/1923 Hasan al-Banna was initiated into the Hasafiyya Brotherhood by Shaykh Hasanayn's son and successor when the latter visited Damanhur, and benefited greatly from his teachings. If Shaykh Zahran had shown him the way to translate faith into action, Shaykh ʻAbd al-Wahhab al-Hasafi impressed another lesson on him: to eschew petty squabbles and disputes among brethren, especially in public, and to focus on practical work leading towards piety, *ta ʻat allah*.

In spite of their grave-visiting habits and the miracle stories told by the brethren, both normally seen as indicators of "popular Sufism," the Hasafiyya was considered one of the sober orders. The Hasafis believed in dreams and the power of prayer and Qur'anic recitation, but they tolerated no displays of ecstasy and no mingling of the sexes. His brother Jamal later took pains to affirm that there was never any extremism in Hasan al-Banna (reflecting the well-known principle that there must be no exaggeration in Islam, *la ghuluww fi l-din*), and that with his father and Shaykh Zahran as role models, Hasan developed harmoniously, always maintaining a healthy balance (*Letters*, p. 90). Hasan al-Banna himself emphasized his disapproval of all "deviations" (including those of his own shaykhs), and stressed Shaykh al-Hasafi's habit of giving advice, enjoining good and prohibiting wrong in his dealings with all people irrespective of wealth and power. He did refer to the miracles (*karamat*) Shaykh al-Hasafi's followers talked about, only to say that they did not affect him the way his deeds did, and that the greatest miracle was to spread the call to Islam, *al-da'wa* (*Memoirs*, p. 22).

His studies at Damanhur necessitated no rupture in his life, for he was able to return to al-Mahmudiyya every weekend. In his *Memoirs* Hasan al-Banna describes the schedule of work and study awaiting him there. Though he was not, as the famous saying has it, "a knight during the day and a monk during the night," he nevertheless worked in his father's shop during the day and spent the evening with his Hasafi brethren. In the course of these activities, he also saw his family and friends, first and foremost Ahmad al-Sukkari. Continuing an earlier pattern, Hasan and his friends did not just work on improving their own character, observing silence, and fasting on Mondays and Thursdays, but they also tended to the conduct of others. At school in Damanhur as well as in al-Mahmudiyya, they called their fellow Muslims to prayer, a task that filled al-Banna with immense satisfaction and a hidden sense of power.

In al-Mahmudiyya, they set up a Hasafi Benevolent Society (al-Jam'iyya al-Khayriyya al-Hasafiyya), with al-Sukkari as president and al-Banna as secretary, which represented a cross between a "regular" Sufi lodge and a voluntary association of a more modern type.

Hasan al-Banna later declared the Hasafi Benevolent Society to be the nucleus or forerunner of the Society of the Muslim Brothers (*Memoirs*, p. 24). Their aims were to call people to what they considered "Islamic morality," to correct wrongs such as alcohol, gambling and un-Islamic funerary customs, and to fight against Christian missionaries, at that time in the guise of three young girls from the evangelical Bible mission headed by a certain Miss White, a fight later taken up by the Muslim Brothers and an enduring concern of Islamic activists.[5]

AT DAR AL-'ULUM

In 1923, when he was not yet seventeen, Hasan al-Banna graduated from the Damanhur elementary teachers' training school, the best of his class. A number of his fellow students decided to move on to Dar al-'Ulum in Cairo. For some time he was uncertain whether to continue on the path of learning, as he put it – and he loved learning, including classical Arabic poetry and prose. But al-Ghazali's *Revival of Religious Sciences* (*Ihya' 'ulum al-din*), which he had read with one of his teachers, who was also a Hasafi, taught him to distinguish between useful and useless knowledge, and to appreciate the virtues of time management (suggesting an Islamic parallel to the utilitarian spirit of al-Banna's own time). Muhammad 'Abduh and Rashid Rida, too, had advocated practical studies combined with true Islam, and al-Banna was a diligent reader of *al-Manar*. Knowledge, he later agreed with his friend al-Sukkari, was a form of *jihad*. But was it really knowledge he was pursuing by seeking a higher degree, or was it fame and self-promotion? After some agonized soul-searching he was persuaded by a trusted teacher at least to take the entrance examination for Dar al-'Ulum.

Equipped with his father's blessings and a letter to one of his father's bookdealer friends in Cairo, Hasan al-Banna set out on his first trip to the capital. The bookdealer took little notice of the young man, and Shaykh Ahmad was not yet sufficiently well established in the scholarly world to pull more powerful strings. Hasan passed the required medical exam and then spent an entire week in the courts of al-Azhar preparing for the entrance examination for Dar al-'Ulum. During the summer breaks he had studied with a shaykh in al-Mahmudiyya, reading Ibn Malik's *al-Khulasa al-alfiyya* with the commentary of Ibn 'Aqil (d. 1367), one of the most popular books on Arabic grammar, written in verse, as well as other books of Hadith and jurisprudence. Even so, he was afraid of grammar, which he had not been able to learn as systematically as had the Azharites, over the course of their eight years of study for their *ahliyya* degrees. In his state of anxiety, he reports, he obtained help from a higher source: the questions were revealed to him in a dream, and he successfully passed the examination, which consisted partly of recitation from memory of sections of the Qur'an and the *Alfiyya* (*Memoirs*, pp. 33f., 42f.). Shortly thereafter, the al-Buhayra governorate offered him an appointment as teacher in a village school near al-Mahmudiyya. Upon reflection he declined the offer in order to study in Cairo, where not only Dar al-'Ulum but also the headquarters of the Hasafiyya Brotherhood were located.

Dar al-'Ulum was founded in 1872 in the reign of Khedive Isma'il by the renowned reformer 'Ali Pasha Mubarak, then minister of education, to train Azhar students and graduates as teachers for the new government primary schools. By the time al-Banna entered Dar al-'Ulum, there were few alternatives to government employment for the educated urban middle class, generally known as the *efendiyya*. In the private sector, foreigners and local foreign minorities – that is, non-Muslims of non-Egyptian background, the majority of whom were foreign subjects or stateless – still predominated. Meanwhile, the state civil service grew from 15,000 permanent positions in 1915 to 42,000 in 1940, accompanied by a gradual replacement of foreigners by Egyptians in the middle and upper ranks. To meet the rising demand for qualified Arabic teachers, Dar al-'Ulum was expanded in the 1920s and its graduates were virtually assured of employment – one of the reasons for enduring tension with al-Azhar, whose graduates gradually lost their monopoly on these positions. As at al-Azhar, the faculty and student body of Dar al-'Ulum were all male and all Muslim. Tuition was free and students received a monthly allowance.

In its outward form and teaching methods Dar al-'Ulum was modern, that is to say patterned on Western models: it had a fixed curriculum, set classes and examinations, classrooms, blackboards, benches and textbooks. In terms of content, the verdict is less clear-cut: the four-year course provided higher education in "traditional" religious subjects and elementary education in "modern" subjects. Dar al-'Ulum put strong emphasis on Arabic and religious studies (Hanafi *fiqh*, Hadith and Qur'anic exegesis, or *tafsir*), but also integrated modern subjects into its curriculum, notably history, geography, mathematics, science, pedagogy and foreign languages. For this reason, the instruction was considered modern in comparison with al-Azhar, but traditional when compared with non-religious institutions of higher learning, such as Cairo University, which had opened in 1925 as successor to the private Egyptian University, founded in 1908. This combination carried the risk of not being recognized by either the traditional or the modern. Taha Husayn (1889–1973) for instance, one of the great literary figures of the twentieth century, who as a talented young blind man from the countryside started out at al-Azhar but transferred to Cairo University as soon as he could, remarked that "its alumni stand uncomfortably suspended, as it were, between the old knowledge and the new, ill-prepared to teach either" (quoted from Reid, *Cairo University*, p. 144).

Hasan al-Banna, however, appreciated the education he received at Dar al-'Ulum. His *Memoirs* contain a lively description of the first lesson he attended, on Arabic poetry and warfare, a combination that was to remain a lasting passion. As a boy he had become enchanted with Arabic tales of love, chivalry and devotion, with their glorification of *jihad* and noble warfare, such as the romance of *Princess Dhat al-Himma*; he also loved nationalist songs and poems. He was later to say that increasingly the young were reading weak literature, which needed to be replaced by stronger literature, extolling the virtues of warfare and self-sacrifice, to give proper guidance to the new generation. As for the rest of his course of study, he did not take any English classes and in fact never learned any foreign language, though he was acquainted with contemporary European thought through Arabic translations.

THE IMPACT OF THE CAPITAL

In Cairo, Hasan al-Banna was exposed to a different social and cultural environment from what he had previously known. In the beginning he shared lodgings with friends in the Sayyida Zaynab area. After his first year at Dar al-'Ulum, his family joined him in Cairo. Shaykh Ahmad's parents had both died that same year, and the idea was to send Hasan's younger brothers to secondary school, an option not available at al-Mahmudiyya: 'Abd al-Rahman enrolled at the Higher School of Commerce and Muhammad at the Religious Institute of al-Azhar. Expenses were considerable, and their mother sold some of her gold jewellery to help cover the costs. Hasan al-Banna was part of the large population of rural migrants to the city, yet he does not seem to have felt the effects of migration the way his parents did. For one thing, Damanhur had already introduced him to an urban lifestyle. Also his connections with the countryside were not cut off, for during the summer breaks he returned to al-Mahmudiyya, his friend al-Sukkari and the Hasafi brethren, justifying the expense (and his absence too) by setting up a watch repair shop there. According to his own testimony, he enjoyed being independent, working with his hands and earning his own money.

The Hasafiyya Brotherhood served as an important link between al-Mahmudiyya, Damanhur and Cairo, providing him with a network of friends and trusted authorities. He derived much pleasure from attending the weekly meeting (*hadra*) of the Hasafi brothers in Cairo, held after Friday prayer in the home of Shaykh al-Hasafi and on other nights in the home of his deputy. At the same time, he engaged with the Hasafis in al-Mahmudiyya, who continued their struggle against foreign missionaries who at that time were stepping up their activities in the area.

The 1920s were a period of intense intellectual and political strife in Egypt, yet we see little of it in al-Banna's letters and *Memoirs*. The social changes and disruptions in the wake of the First World War left their imprint on Egyptian society. This was the heyday of party politics in Egypt, with the Wafd and the Liberal Constitutionalists playing leading roles, and politics was freely discussed at school. Religious matters were also debated, and the students frequently disagreed with their professors. Hasan al-Banna was a serious young man, and eager to learn. Part of his free time was spent at libraries and bookstores where he bought books with the monthly stipend paid by Dar al-'Ulum to its students and the money he earned at the shop. In striking contrast to Sayyid Qutb, who with a similar background and education moved in rather exciting literary circles, Hasan al-Banna seems to have taken little part in the cultural and intellectual life of the capital. If his *Memoirs* are to be trusted, he never went to the theatre or a concert, not to mention casinos, clubs, music halls or the cinema. Nor is there any indication of any more patently sinful entertainment.

Thus it cannot have been participant observation that aroused his moral indignation or outright disgust, for disgusted he was by what he registered in his new environment: licentiousness, immorality, the so-called liberation of women and "democracy." In 1924 the caliphate was abolished in Turkey and in 1925 Cairo University was transformed into a state university, a secular institution "revolting against religion," whose teachers and students, he declared, were unfettered nihilists and libertarians (*Memoirs*, pp. 53f.). He seems to have forgotten that he himself had been largely educated in the government school system and was preparing to join it as a teacher. In his tract *Between Yesterday and Today*, he was later to write that the Europeans:[6]

> brought their half-naked women into these regions [the Orient], their liquors, their theatres, their dance halls, their entertainments, their stories, their newspapers, their romances, their phantasies, their frivolous pastimes and their insolent jokes. Here they countenanced crimes they did not tolerate in their own countries, and decked out this boisterous, frivolous world, reeking with sin and redolent with

> vice, to the eyes of the simple-minded deluded Muslims of wealth and influence, and to those of rank and power. They were not satisfied until they had founded schools and scientific and cultural institutions in the very heart of the Islamic realm, which cast doubt and heresy into the souls of its sons and taught them how to demean themselves, disparage their religion and their fatherland, divest themselves of their traditions and beliefs, and to regard as sacred anything Western, in the belief that only what came from the Europeans could serve as the supreme model to be emulated in this life.

It should be said that the "dissolution of morals" was not solely due to foreign influence, though it is true that during the First World War British and Australian soldiers stationed in Egypt had openly defied social conventions, and that certain Europeans resident in the country exploited their privileged legal status under the Capitulations to traffick in women, an enterprise known as *La traite des blanches*. But much of what Hasan al-Banna reacted to was not alien to Egyptian society: music, dance and singing, coffeehouses, even gambling, alcohol, drugs and prostitution. Al-Azhar itself was not far from al-Azbakiyya, the main entertainment district in town. But this was not what al-Banna perceived (*Memoirs*, p. 54):

> I was deeply pained, for I saw that the social life of the beloved Egyptian nation was oscillating between its dear and precious Islam, which it had inherited, protected, lived with and taken pride in for fourteen entire centuries, and this violent Western aggression (*ghazw*), armed and equipped with all the deadly material weapons of money, status, outward appearance, indulgence, power and the means of propaganda.

Characteristically, he translated his malaise into action, both individually and more importantly in a group of like-minded young men. In 1924, al-Banna joined the Society for the Noble Islamic Virtues (Jam'iyyat Makarim al-Akhlaq al-Islamiyya), which in the tradition of charitable associations working in the field of education and moral betterment held weekly public lectures. According to him it was the only Islamic association to be found in Cairo at the time.

This is not correct, for there were a number of other Islamic societies active at the time, male as well as female, including the Islamic Benevolent Society (al-Jam'iyya al-Khayriyya al-Islamiyya), and the Shari'a Society (al-Jam'iyya al-Shar'iyya).

It was then that the idea of training a group of young men seems to have come up, men who would preach in public venues such as clubs and coffeehouses and attract people to (true) Islam. Though it is difficult to prove a direct link, it is worthy of note that at the time American and British Protestant missionaries already used preaching in coffeehouses and public bars to spread the gospel (Sharkey, *American Evangelicals*, pp. 105–7). Al-Banna's friends were sceptical when they first discussed the idea but willing to give it a try. So during Ramadan they went from one coffeehouse to the other, altogether some twenty establishments in one single night, where al-Banna gave short "sermons" (*khutba*) of five or ten minutes each, which were well received. By his own account, coffeehouse preaching had been his idea and initiative. When the conflict with Ahmad al-Sukkari erupted in the late 1940s, the latter's friends credited al-Sukkari with the idea and claimed that it was originally linked to the Hasafiyya Brotherhood. There is certainly a danger of making al-Banna the pivot of all the associations he belonged to, projecting his later prominence on to the earlier stages of his career.

In Cairo, Hasan al-Banna also gained better access to Islamic intellectuals, scholars and activists than he had previously enjoyed as a student in a provincial town. To be admitted to their circles, he needed *wasta* – patronage and protection – and this was in part provided by men his father was in touch with, such as Muhibb al-Din al-Khatib and Muhammad Farid Wajdi.[7] Wajdi Bey (1875–1954) was a disciple of Abduh's and editor of the journal *al-Hayat*; in 1908 his wife, Fatima Rashid, had founded the first women's association in Egypt which also issued a journal, to propagate women's rights within an Islamic framework. It appears, however, that for Hasan al-Banna the Sufi link was still of major importance. Thus contact with Shaykh Yusuf al-Dijwi (1870–1946), a prominent Azhar shaykh and one of the chief opponents of both 'Ali 'Abd al-Raziq and Rashid

Rida, was made through their common attachment to Sufism. Al-Banna was familiar with al-Dijwi's work and deliberately sought him out because of his standing in the "Islamic camp," though the shaykh ultimately proved a disappointment. Not so Muhibb al-Din al-Khatib (1886–1969), the prominent Syrian journalist-cum-activist and "cultural entrepreneur" (to use Glaß's term) of the Arab renaissance, or *nahda*, who had moved to Cairo in the early 1920s. Al-Khatib ran a publishing house and bookshop, Dar al-Matba'a al-Salafiyya and al-Maktaba al-Salafiyya, which served as an important forum for reform-minded circles intent on defending Islam and fighting Westernization (*tafarnuj*). Interestingly, Rashid Rida does not figure prominently in the pages of al-Banna's *Memoirs* – either he was too busy and important for a young student, or al-Banna was aware of Rida's hostility to "popular" Sufism, which, for him, included the Shadhiliyya order in general and the "grave-worshippers" (*al-quburiyyun*) in particular, of whom al-Banna was one.

In June 1926, in the wake of heated debate over the abolition of the caliphate, al-Khatib and his associates created the journal *al-Fath* (*Opening*, *Conquest*), an initiative that, in characteristic fashion, al-Banna later traced to himself. According to him, it all began one evening at the house of Shaykh al-Dijwi, who had basically given up the struggle. Al-Banna challenged him and gave a fiery speech on the duty to fight for Islam: the people are with us for this is a Muslim people, the forces of evil will not win, but al-Azhar will have to stand up, and so on. Several of the shaykhs present felt he had misbehaved vis-à-vis al-Dijwi. Later in the evening he gave an even more militant speech at somebody else's home: Islam is fighting a fierce war and its leaders are not there. Don't you believe God will hold you accountable? Some of those present were moved to tears. Out of this came the journal *al-Fath* and, later, the Society of the Muslim Brothers. The anecdote could be read as the "framing" of his youthful enthusiasm as *kalimat haqq*, "speaking truth in the face of the mighty," confirming al-Banna in his role as counsellor and earnest "warner" – telling, not as a statement of fact, but as an instance of self-projection and quite possibly self-perception as well. *Al-Fath* was combative and polemical, committed to the defence of Islam and what it considered Islamic morality; it also fought many of the socio-cultural "ills" al-Banna and the Muslim Brothers were later to attack – but it was not al-Banna's creation.

Hasan al-Banna graduated from Dar al-'Ulum in June 1927. The examination was largely based on rote learning and he knew a large quantity of Arabic poetry by heart. Because of his good marks, al-Banna was able to apply for an educational mission abroad, and after some hesitation did so. Briefly he even considered studying in a country outside the Islamic world. He was spared the decision as Dar al-'Ulum did not nominate any of its graduates for foreign service in 1927. His hopes that he would be appointed to Cairo were dashed. To his dismay, he was assigned as Arabic teacher to a primary school in Isma'iliyya in the Suez Canal Zone, a place he could not even locate on the map. His protest, however, was in vain. A friend told him that the town was calm and pleasant, and when he consulted his father, Shaykh Ahmad said it was God's will.

THE SOCIETY OF THE MUSLIM BROTHERS: 1928–38

PLANTING THE SEED IN ISMA‘ILIYYA

Hasan al-Banna started his post in September 1927 filled with high hopes and expectations. In a school essay he had made a "covenant" with God to engage in *da‘wa* to spread true Islam. He was now almost twenty-one years old, and this was to be his mission in life.[1] After forty days spent successively at a hotel and two boarding houses run by European ladies, he and some friends rented a flat. The arrangement he reports is remarkable, representing as it does the evolution of the three monotheistic faiths: the ground floor was occupied by Jews, the first floor by Christians, and the top floor by al-Banna and his Muslim friends. Al-Banna proved a conscientious teacher who took his vocation seriously. In 1928, for instance, he did not visit his parents for the Breaking of the Fast at the end of Ramadan (*‘id al-fitr*) because the students had to prepare for their examinations. He was also a conscientious son and brother: with his salary of fifteen Egyptian pounds per month, which was substantial by contemporary standards, he was able to support his family with a monthly payment of three to five pounds, and in addition took care of several of his younger siblings who stayed with him for extended periods of time.

In his methodical fashion, Hasan al-Banna set about becoming acquainted with his new surroundings and identifying the social groups to be targeted if he wished to spread the call among his fellow

Muslims. Again, his Sufi affiliation seems to have been of use. In the late 1920s, Isma'iliyya hosted the largest British military base in the country, and the administration of the foreign-owned Suez Canal Company was partly located there. As a result, the town was dominated by Europeans, though of its 25,000 inhabitants only one-tenth were foreigners, mainly Italian and French citizens. As in other colonial cities, the foreigners lived next to but clearly separate from the Egyptian populace – a situation that did not fail to leave its mark on Hasan al-Banna, with his keen awareness of social issues. At the same time, he was put off by the clannishness of local Muslim society, which was divided into rival groups and parties, most of them tied to personal and family interests. Though he was later to say that the mosque was the people's university, he resolved to stay away from the mosques with their petty squabbles, and to reach out to a wider audience that did not frequent them.

In consequence, al-Banna turned once again to coffeehouse preaching. He selected three large establishments and went to each twice a week. There he stood on a chair and spoke, but never for more than ten minutes. In order not to alienate his listeners, he did not harp on what they did wrong, which would have included the very fact that they were sitting in a coffeehouse, a venue that for centuries had been denounced in pious circles as a site of idleness and immorality. Neither did he evoke hellfire and other punishments. Rather, he focused on what might draw the audience to Islam, emphasizing the "ease" of Islam (*yusr al-islam*), telling stories and anecdotes and speaking partly in the Egyptian dialect. This constituted a clear departure from his youthful days, when he and his friends had castigated people for their transgressions, real or alleged (though even then they had avoided direct confrontation and resorted to letters and denunciations to the authorities instead). People were not used to seeing a young man who did not look like a religious scholar or talk like one speak to them of Islam. They found it strange, but they did not run away. Still, the impact of coffeehouse preaching, novel though it was, must not be overrated: it created a fleeting impression that may have made some people desirous to learn more about "true" Islam, but did not create a real momentum, let alone a permanent structure.

In addition to these coffeehouse ventures, al-Banna wrote articles for the Cairo-based journal *al-Fath*, trying to win subscribers in Isma'iliyya. When in November 1927 he learned about the creation of the Young Men's Muslim Association (YMMA, Jam'iyyat al-Shubban al-Muslimin), with ties to the anti-British National Party (al-Hizb al-Watani) and its pan-Islamic orientation, he immediately joined it. Here we encounter the connection between patriotism and religious reform that was to become the hallmark of the Muslim Brotherhood and other Islamist groups.

Slowly he made an impact, especially on young men of modest background. In spring 1928, some six months after his arrival in Isma'iliyya, he felt ready to move one step further and set up an association of his own. Hasan al-Banna may well have been marked by a single-minded purpose and endowed with remarkable willpower and energy, combined with uncommon social skills and a prodigious memory, especially for names and faces. Yet his group started from modest beginnings and it evolved slowly. There is still some dispute regarding its foundation and links to existing organizations, notably the Hasafiyya Brotherhood and the YMMA, links which both ran through al-Banna. He later gave a vivid account of the first meeting, which obtained the status of a foundation myth. According to him, six men turned to him in March 1928 with an earnest plea (*Memoirs*, p. 76):

> We listened and became aware and felt the impact [of your teaching]. [But] We do not know the practical way to attain the glory of Islam and the welfare of the Muslims. We are weary of this life of humiliation and captivity. Indeed, you see that the Arabs and the Muslims in this country have no status or dignity. They are but hirelings depending on these foreigners. We own nothing except the blood that flows hot with pride in our veins, a spirit that overflows with faith and honour, and these few coins from our children's sustenance. We are unable to perceive the road to action as you perceive it, or to know the path to serve the fatherland, religion and community as you know it. All we

> desire now is to offer you all we possess, to be acquitted by God of the responsibility, and for you to be responsible for us and for what we must do before him. A group that earnestly pledges unto God that they will live for his religion and die for it, desiring nothing but his face, is worthy of victory though their numbers be small and weak.

All he could do was to accept the burden and solemnly pledge with them (*nubayi ʿallah*) that they would be "soldiers (*jund*) for the Islamic call, which encompassed the life of the fatherland and the glory of the community." The brief passage is rich in meaning, offering, as Richard Mitchell has remarked, a "highly dramatized but very accurate summing-up of the inspiration and spirit of the movement" (*Society*, p. 8). By his own account, al-Banna was chosen and appointed as leader (*imam*) by a small group of devoted Muslims. In religious circles it has always been important not to be thought to be seeking power, but to be sought out by others and charged with guidance and leadership, a repository of trust. What we see is a conscious modelling on the pious forefathers (*al-salaf al-salih*), and the Rightly Guided Caliphs more specifically, in a kind of modernized succession (*istikhlaf*). Equally significant is the language of patriotism, *jihad* and sacrifice for the sake of the fatherland and the Muslim community.

The story also sheds light on the name the group adopted: were they to think of themselves as a society or a club, a Sufi brotherhood or a trade union? No, he said, none of these: "We are brothers in the service of Islam. Hence we are the 'Muslim Brothers'" (*Memoirs*, p. 76). In the following years it became difficult to separate the man from the movement he founded and to a large degree embodied, the Society of the Muslim Brothers (Jamʿiyyat al-Ikhwan al-Muslimin), or Muslim Brotherhood for short; frequently the Muslim Brothers were simply referred to as "the Ikhwan."

Against a backdrop of colonial rule, the Muslim Brothers aimed at providing an Islamic education (*tarbiya*) and moral orientation (*tahdhib*) to their members and a wider public, in order to make them "understand Islam correctly." Education and the call, or mission, *daʿwa*, were thus intimately linked. Islamic education was a core concern of the Salafi reformers in Egypt, Syria and Iraq who had observed the educational activities of Christian missionaries from Europe and America with a mixture of admiration and apprehension. In 1911–12, Rashid Rida had opened his Dar al-Da'wa wa-l-Irshad, a school to train teachers and preachers (who were called guides, *murshids*) independently of al-Azhar, but was forced to close it at the outbreak of the First World War. Education was the defining concern of Islamic modernism in India, and educated circles in Egypt were acquainted with its major features. Aligarh for instance was known through the Arabic press and Rashid Rida had even visited India. Egyptians may have been less well informed about the evolving Islamic mass movements in what is today Indonesia – first and foremost the Muhammadiyah, founded in 1912, and Nahdlatul Ulama, created in 1926, which also put heavy emphasis on Islamic education. But this was something different: Hasan al-Banna was in many ways a new man and of a different type from the reform-minded thinkers and activists who, at least in his native Egypt, had almost exclusively been either *'ulama'* or journalists or both. He and his friends ultimately took Islamic education beyond the mosque, the school and the press, and linked it to larger social and political concerns, giving it new shape and momentum.

From the outset, Hasan al-Banna made it a principle to focus on issues with a potential to unite Muslims rather than to divide them: instruction in the true nature of Islam, social justice, the struggle against immorality and the fight against Christian missionaries. It was only from the mid-1930s onwards that national liberation, anti-imperialism and the defence of the Islamic homeland featured more prominently on the agenda. The Muslim Brothers were able to move among Islamic personalities and institutions, first and foremost the mosques, and to use religious events and celebrations, from Friday prayer to the pilgrimage to Mecca, to reach out to a wider audience. If ultimately they proved more successful than others, it was largely because of the attention they paid to recruiting adherents, mentoring members and fostering a group spirit.

In the beginning, the Muslim Brothers rented a room in an office building for meetings and evening classes, and launched a programme of Islamic studies that was largely if not exclusively taught by al-Banna himself. Called Madrasat al-Tahdhib, it focused on the basics: correct Qur'anic recitation and the memorization of Qur'anic verse and selected Hadiths with some commentary, supplemented by instruction on the creed and religious obligations, the life of the Prophet and his companions as well as elements of Islamic history. The programme was designed to train preachers or missionaries rather than scholars: there was to be no allegorical interpretation, learned digression or philosophical reflection. The correspondence of this programme with colonial visions of useful education for the lower classes is too striking to be passed over, though the ultimate goal was radically different. By the end of the first year, some seventy men had attended the classes – the first cohort (*al-ra'il al-awwal*) as they came to be known.

And yet, when, towards the end of 1928, the opportunity presented itself, Hasan al-Banna was prepared to leave Isma'iliyya and move to Mecca to teach at a religious institution there. Hijaz had recently been annexed by Ibn Sa'ud, and his adviser Hafiz Wahba contacted the Young Men's Muslim Association to recruit teachers. Muhibb al-Din al-Khatib asked al-Banna whether he would be ready to go, and he was. Eventually, the project came to nothing because the Egyptian government did not recognize the Sa'udi kingdom of Najd and Hijaz established in 1926, and as a government employee Hasan al-Banna did not dare to defy official policies.

CONTESTATION AND SUSPICION

Even at this early stage, Hasan al-Banna was not uncontroversial. There were people who contested his positions, questioned his scholarship and suspected his motives. Some focused on his Sufi leanings rather than his leadership of the small and insignificant group of Muslim Brothers. Under the impact of reform Islam, and Rashid Rida more particularly, many aspects of Sufism had come under attack. Hasan al-Banna made no secret of his attachment to

Sufism and certain practices, such as visiting graves and tombs, that many perceived as "popular" or outright blameworthy. Sufism was very much alive in Isma'iliyya, and al-Banna frequented several orders and lodges, although he took care not to appear as partisan to the Hasafiyya Brotherhood, so as not to compromise the "general call." So, people asked, what did the *ustadh* think about *tawassul*, the intercession of saints? Hasan al-Banna was not amused by the question. He lashed out against dispute and strife tearing the Muslim community apart and told the questioners to ask a scholar if they wanted to know more about these matters. He was merely a schoolteacher who had memorized a few Qur'anic verses, Hadiths and legal rulings. Muslims, he told them, should move beyond secondary issues such as the different ways of praying. They should be tolerant, respect the views of others and unite on what truly mattered. At the same time, certain Muslim scholars objected to certain opinions that reflected a reformist, rational reading of the sources, such as his suggestion that the Prophet's night journey should be seen as a spiritual experience rather than a physical voyage. Interestingly and, as it was to turn out, characteristically, al-Banna resolved to avoid conflict, especially over what could be broadly defined as theological issues, and to give the scholars the scholars' due. For the time being he did not insist on his views, even though he continued to uphold them in the 1940s.

His activities brought him to the attention of local notables, including a judge at the religious court and some well-to-do merchants and businessmen, who gave his fledgling organization the financial and moral support it needed if it were to prosper and grow. The strategy of courting the elite required some justification which al-Banna provided by stressing his role as counsellor and moral guide, pointing out the right path to the leaders of the community. He also gave a number of talks at a workers' club and a temperance society. The activities of another member of the Society, Shaykh Muhammad Farghali, among workers in a gypsum factory proved more risky. According to al-Banna, Farghali helped to lift the workers out of their lowly condition and to develop a sense of self-respect as God's deputies on earth (*khulafa' allah*). The company suspected the preacher of communism and made attempts to fire him. Eventually, a compromise was reached that allowed both sides to save face.

From the beginning, Hasan al-Banna paid close attention to enhancing the public visibility and corporate identity of his group. In the early phase, weekly meetings were modelled on a Sufi *hadra*, with Sufi chants, processions, banners and similar paraphernalia in evidence. The first major project was to build a mosque. The Muslim Brothers were not the only ones to engage in mosque building in Isma'iliyya; at least two other projects were underway at about the same time. Given al-Banna's comments on the clannishness of local society, it is significant that he should set up a mosque of his own, though one not linked to a prominent family clan. Al-Banna first demanded that members contribute from their own money. One Muslim Brother reportedly even sold his bicycle to meet his obligations. It helped that in close cooperation with the ministry of interior, al-Azhar had just established an Office for Preaching and Guidance (Idarat al-Wa'z wa-l-Irshad) and assigned al-Banna's friend Hamid 'Askariyya to Isma'iliyya. 'Askariyya fought a heroic struggle, calling for contributions to the mosque in his Friday sermons and even visiting people at home.

To attract third-party donations, the Society of the Muslim Brothers had to acquire legal status as a registered welfare association, and did so in 1930. As a consequence, it was legally banned from engaging in politics. Funds came from wealthy donors such as a contractor who lent 500 Egyptian pounds, and the Suez Canal Company, which offered the same sum. The mosque was opened in February 1931 on the *laylat al-qadr*, the "night of power," when, according to Sura 97.1, the Qur'an was sent down, which in this particular year coincided with the anniversary of the battle of Badr in which the Muslim community had won its first victory over its Meccan foes in 2/624.

Shortly after, a club was added, as was a school for boys, called Islamic Hira' Institute (Ma'had Hira' al-Islami), after the cave on Mount Hira', near Mecca, where Muhammad had received the first revelation. To emphasize its Islamic character at a time when

European ideas on education were the fashion – as a schoolteacher, al-Banna was well acquainted with the theories of Montessori, Pestalozzi and others – and Christian missionaries were actively promoting their educational theories, the Muslim Brothers designed a schedule that was adjusted to the prayer rhythm and a distinctive dress consisting of a *jallabiyya*, smock, *tarbush* and sandals, all made in Egypt. This was a time of economic nationalism, fuelled by the Great Depression of 1929–32; in October 1931 the so-called Piastre Plan was created to mobilize national capital and the Muslim Brothers thus contributed their share to the national endeavour. The school offered a three-tiered programme: one prepared students to enter al-Azhar, another prepared them for secondary school and a third combined basic instruction with vocational training in various handicrafts. Tuition fees were moderate and the atmosphere was free and open, allowing the close bond between teachers and pupils to develop that Hasan al-Banna had cherished in his own school days. In September 1932, a girls' school was added, significantly called School for the Mothers of the Believers (Madrasat Ummahat al-Mu'minin), which equally adopted what al-Banna described as a modern Islamic style (*minhaj 'asri islami*), that is to say a style adapted to the needs and aspirations of the time. It was later taken over by the ministry of education.

Success bred suspicion. Soon there were rumours of hidden agendas, of cheating and of hero-worship among the Ikhwan. Some said that in accepting funding from the Suez Canal Company, the Muslim Brothers had compromised their credibility and revealed themselves as stooges of imperialism. Hasan al-Banna retorted that the 500 Egyptian pounds the Company had offered as a loan was nothing compared to the 500,000 Egyptian pounds it had (allegedly) donated to build a Christian church in town. Petitions were also sent to the authorities claiming that al-Banna was a communist working for Moscow, or alternatively a Wafdist, and that he had publicly said things against the king that did not bear repeating. These were the days of the government of Isma'il Sidqi, a sworn enemy of the Wafd and the left, and such allegations were not to be taken lightly. Another petition, signed by an anonymous "Christian," charged al-Banna with instigating sectarian conflict between Muslims and Christians. In a remarkable move, high-ranking representatives of the local Coptic community formally refuted the charge, lending credibility to al-Banna's claim that the Muslim Brothers made every effort not to alienate the Copts and even actively to seek an understanding with them.

On a different level, a local shaykh spread allegations that al-Banna invited his followers to worship him in the place of God, practising human idolatry, *shirk*, which amounted to heresy. After a formal investigation al-Banna was cleared of all accusations, and the inspector charged with the investigation vowed to join the Muslim Brothers after his retirement (which apparently he did). In characteristic fashion, Hasan al-Banna and authors sympathetic to the Brotherhood later presented the episode as part of a larger pattern of the persecution of the righteous, creating a parallel with what the messengers of God had had to face, culminating with the Prophet himself – forever a role model and a source of comfort, just as the Prophet had taken comfort in the trials and tribulations suffered by the prophets before him.

Activities gradually extended to several towns in the Suez Canal Zone as well as to the eastern Delta. In July 1931, a small Islamic association in Cairo called Islamic Culture Society (Jam'iyyat al-Hadara al-Islamiyya), founded by al-Banna's younger brother 'Abd al-Rahman and a number of his friends, merged with the Muslim Brotherhood. 'Abd al-Rahman had recently graduated from the Higher School of Commerce and was now an employee with the railway steam engine company; his friends were of similar background. Hasan al-Banna decided to subsidize the Cairo branch, which had allegedly rejected offers from the Sidqi government to grant it financial support. These monthly subsidies, however, angered those among the Muslim Brothers in Isma'iliyya who saw no reason to transfer scarce funds to the capital. This led to the first internal crisis over al-Banna's style of leadership. Hasan al-Banna spoke of a conspiracy; his faithful biographers used the highly charged terms of *mihna* and *fitna*. The sense of ill-feeling lasted well beyond the official resolution of the conflict in the summer of 1932.

THE MOVE TO CAIRO

At his own request, Hasan al-Banna was transferred to a primary school in Cairo in October 1932 and shortly after moved the Society's "headquarters" to the capital. The Muslim Brothers in Isma'iliyya were apparently taken by surprise and protested to the ministry on the mistaken assumption that the transfer had occurred against his will. In his last year in Isma'iliyya, in the midst of the internal crisis, Hasan al-Banna had married.[2] The *Memoirs* contain only a passing reference with no description of the bride. From other sources we learn that she was chosen by his mother from a pious merchant family living in comfortable circumstances, who later occasionally supported him financially. The bride reportedly was of light complexion but not very pretty, lively but forced to reign in her liveliness as the future wife of a preacher. She created a stable atmosphere for him, free of female temptation (*fitnat al-nisa'*). Some said he could have done better in terms of (her) beauty, money or education, but that was not what he required to fulfil his mission. Witness the saying attributed to the Prophet: "When he looked at her she pleased him, and when he gave her an order she obeyed, and when he was away from her she was true to him." Over the years, she bore al-Banna two sons and six daughters: two of the children died young, and the youngest daughter was born after his assassination and named Istishhad, "The one who seeks martyrdom."

In the beginning, the headquarters of the Muslim Brotherhood occupied the ground floor in a house Hasan al-Banna rented for himself and his growing family as well as his parents and younger siblings, highlighting the close link between the al-Banna family and the Society of the Muslim Brothers. Hasan al-Banna appointed several family members to important positions within the Society: thus his younger brother 'Abd al-Rahman was head of the Cairo branch until he took charge of the Muslim Brothers' printing press; in 1935, he was sent on a mission to Syria. In 1936–7, their father served for a short period as the director of the Muslim Brothers' periodical, and a decade later, Hasan's brother-in-law 'Abd al-Hakim 'Abidin was secretary general of the Muslim Brotherhood.

The following period is usually divided into two phases, the first from his move to Cairo to the outbreak of the Second World War, seven years that saw important changes in Egyptian political and cultural life, and the second from the end of the War to al-Banna's death in February 1949, a period witnessing an unprecedented level of violence in Egyptian domestic politics.

BUILDING A BASE

Salafi leaders such as 'Abduh and Rashid Rida, as well as their Syrian and Iraqi counterparts, had developed new ideas, set up cultural and political associations, opened schools and communicated their views via a thriving press. The Muslim Brothers and Hasan al-Banna more specifically built an organization with solid structures and trained cadres that proved able to survive dramatic personnel changes at the top and to withstand strong external pressure. Ultimately, success rested on three pillars: institution building, indoctrination and the cultivation of personal loyalties both horizontally and vertically. While in the new Cairo base the focus remained on mission, guidance and instruction (*da'wa*, *irshad* and *tarbiya*) activities took a new direction. Significantly, al-Banna did not begin by opening a mosque and a school but focused on outreach and expansion. Among the new elements were Muslim Brother periodicals, "general conferences" and, starting in the late 1930s, regular talks al-Banna gave to the Ikhwan on Tuesdays (known as *Tuesday Talks*, *Hadith al-thalatha'*). In the process, the Society of the Muslim Brothers was gradually transformed from a benevolent society with pronounced Sufi elements to a social movement with the attributes of a mass political party, with certain elements of the cadre party superimposed. Throughout, indoctrination played a much more prominent role than in regular political parties, with instruction being based almost exclusively on Hasan al-Banna's speeches, articles and treatises (*rasa'il*).

To establish their presence in the public arena, the Muslim Brothers had to foster internal cohesion and catch the public eye, for as one scholar observed, "the atmosphere in which communication took place was as important as what was communicated" (Mitchell, *Society*, p. 190). On both accounts they were remarkably successful. The Muslim Brother idiom drew on several registers: Salafi reform, Sufism, Egyptian patriotism and contemporary European ideologies, including fascism; all were interpreted to emphasize the unity of purpose, obedience, devotion and sacrifice of the Muslim Brothers, the Egyptian nation and the Muslim community at large. Marches, rallies, chants and banners allowed the Ikhwan to be seen and heard by a wider public. Special care was taken to create a climate of mutual concern and solidarity among Brothers; visits, tea parties and celebrations, honorific titles, badges and other insignia were all designed to create a corporate identity. In the early years, a silver ring was given to all new members. On certain occasions, members wore a green sash with the name "the Muslim Brothers" written on it. Their emblem, which originally consisted of the crescent with the Qur'an, was later replaced by two crossed swords cradling the Qur'an. In the course of the 1930s the Sufi element was thus supplemented by signs and symbols unique to the Muslim Brotherhood, marking its distinctive identity.

After the transfer to Cairo, regular meetings of the General Consultative Council (Majlis al-Shura al-'Amm) were held, commonly referred to as General Conferences. The first one, held in Isma'iliyya in June 1933, was still on a modest scale. It laid down revised statutes (General Law, *al-qanun al-'amm*) and set up a General Guidance Office (Maktab al-Irshad al-'Amm, MIA) as the highest decision-making body within the Society, which consisted of two Azhar scholars from Cairo, four leading members of the Cairo branch including Hasan al-Banna's brother 'Abd al-Rahman, plus, as associates, four Muslim Brothers representing provincial branches, all of them appointed by Hasan al-Banna. The General Guidance Office was thus largely identical with the Cairo branch, reflecting Egypt's tradition of bureaucratic centralization. In response to internal critique, it was later separated from the Cairo branch and made into an independent body. The Second General Conference was held in Port Said in January 1934 and decided, among other things, to establish a printing press. The General Law was revised by al-Banna and adopted at the Third General Conference in March 1935. It clearly confirmed his leadership role as the Muslim Brothers' "General Guide" (*al-murshid al-'amm*). In October 1935, new headquarters were acquired in a lower-middle-class neighbourhood in the Sayyida Zaynab quarter of Cairo. The building, however, was still rather unattractive. The move, in 1937, to new headquarters in 'Ataba Square on the fringes of modern Cairo signified a gradual rise in status.

The Muslim Brothers portrayed themselves as the voice of Islam and the Egyptian people. The people speaking for "the people" (*al-sha'b*) belonged mostly to the urban (lower) middle class of Egyptian origin; they were predominantly Muslim, educated in state schools and used to the basic features of modern living. Researchers have highlighted the character of the Muslim Brotherhood as a non-elite (*ahli, sha'bi*) movement with a popular base, style and agenda, which appealed to the educated middle class (*efendiyya*), which in Egypt was seen as very much part of "the people." Scholars have even spoken of the "Islam of the *efendiyya*," the white-collar professional class, both salaried and self-employed, comprising the bulk of the professionals and civil servants plus the petty bourgeoisie, that is to say artisans, shopkeepers, small-scale traders and the owners of small industry.[3]

"*Efendiyya*" designates a class, though not one defined by its control of the means of production, and it refers not just to socio-economic status, but also to the adoption of certain ideas and modes of behaviour that were commonly, if vaguely, defined as "modern" by contemporaries and later observers alike. It is important to stress that "modern" is not synonymous with profoundly Westernized or infatuated with Western ways, the type ridiculed by Rashid Rida and others as *mutafarnij* (from *ifranji*, Frankish, Western) and identified with godlessness and cultural alienation. Hasan al-Banna, *efendi* that he was through his education, occupation and lifestyle, serves to illustrate the point. In contrast to other social movements and political parties, the Muslim Brothers were able also to reach out to urban workers and segments of the rural population, though as their programme required a certain level of literacy they did not manage to recruit large numbers of peasants.

By and large, the Muslim Brotherhood was a movement of lower- and lower-middle-class males – *young* middle-class males. Hasan al-Banna himself was a young man, having just reached his mid-twenties, and he appealed to men of his age and background. In his tract *To Youth*, dated 1357/1938, he stated that the success of the Islamic mission rested on four pillars – firm belief, sincere devotion, zeal and action – and that these qualities could only be found among the young (*Rasa'il*, p. 71). When he said "youth," he meant men. It is true that some attention was also given to women, first and foremost the wives and relatives of the Ikhwan, for whom a Muslim Sister Group (Firqat al-Akhawat al-Muslimat) was set up in Isma'iliyya in April 1933, which was connected to the girls' school. Similar groups emerged in Cairo and Port Said. But up to the end of the Second World War, the Muslim Sisters saw little development, and certainly nothing resembling the growth of the male section, partly because of resistance on the part of the Muslim Brothers themselves.[4]

In the 1930s, the majority of active members were men in their early twenties who claimed their right to participate in public affairs in the name of Islam. Many of them were first-generation immigrants to the cities, educated in government schools. For them, the Muslim Brotherhood seemed to offer a vision that bridged the gap between the Islam they knew from their hometowns and villages and modern life as experienced in the larger cities. In spite of his emphasis on the popular basis of the Muslim Brothers, al-Banna was especially interested in recruiting students. Thus he reportedly said that a student from one of the universities would be more useful to the Islamic mission than a whole village.[5] In 1933, six students were sworn in to form a Student Section, which by 1936 had grown to perhaps 100–200 members. It may be a coincidence that, like the original nucleus of the Society of the Muslim Brothers, it is again the number six that should be mentioned in the sources. Even more striking is the fact that the six allegedly represented the major faculties in Egyptian universities and institutes of higher learning: language and literature (*adab*), medicine, natural sciences, law, agriculture and the Higher School of Commerce; only the technical sciences were not yet represented.

The Student Section often served as the forum where al-Banna presented his policy statements. In the autumn of 1939, he decided to supplement his *Tuesday Talks* in Cairo with *Thursday Talks* directed at a student audience. By 1940, the Committee for Student Affairs, the successor of the Student Section, was the single largest and most articulate section within the Brotherhood. It should be noted, however, that the Muslim Brothers achieved their best results in secondary schools, not at King Fu'ad (Cairo) University or Dar al-'Ulum, where they faced strong competition from political rivals.

The 1930s were a time of "youthful disenchantment with the professional politicians" (Abdalla, *Student Movement*, p. 42), and at least in the cities, the Muslim Brothers had to make an effort to be seen and heard among the host of clubs, groups and parties claiming to speak for Egyptian youth. In the early 1930s, the Young Men's Muslim Association was the largest and most prestigious Islamic organization in Egypt. Its leadership was made up of older men of elite status, who received substantial subsidies from members of the royal family and discouraged political activities among the rank and file. Already in 1928 it had opened branches in Palestine, Syria and Iraq. Hasan al-Banna was a member and able to publish in its monthly *Majallat al-Shubban al-Muslimin* and to give a number of lectures at the YMMA clubhouse in Cairo.

If the Muslim Brothers' relationship with the YMMA could be characterized as one of cooperation, their relationship with Young Egypt (Misr al-Fatat), an openly political group, was always defined by competition. Young Egypt was founded in October 1933 by Ahmad Husayn and Fathi Radwan – both born in 1911 and thus five years younger than Hasan al-Banna – as an association that claimed the heroic days of 1919 as its heritage, when in the aftermath of the First World War the Egyptian people had risen against British occupation, a heritage that had so far been identified with the Wafd. The Wafd continued to stress the unity of the Egyptian nation, comprising Muslims and Copts, and represented by the crescent and the cross. Young Egypt adopted a more militant brand of Egyptian nationalism which put greater emphasis on its Islamic character: under the slogans "God, country and king," "Egypt above all" and "glory to Egypt," it opposed any kind of foreign interference and the adoption of "immoral" and "un-Islamic" practices of foreign origin, such as gambling, alcohol and prostitution. Ahmad Husayn's main work was significantly called *My Faith* (*Imani*). Young Egypt's social base was distinctly urban and included students and young workers in Alexandria, Cairo, Port Said and the provinces, though its membership always remained relatively small in number. Young Egypt was also distinguished by its military features and its emphasis on discipline, law and order; active members were called *mujahids* (those engaged in *jihad*), who formed battalions, brigades and corps, and in 1934, a paramilitary youth organization called the Green Shirts (al-Qumsan al-Khadra') was set up, headed by a Jihad General Staff Council.

In spite of their demonstrative reference to lower-class members, the Muslim Brothers in general and Hasan al-Banna in particular always remained keen to obtain the goodwill of community leaders. The aim was to gain respectability and to reach out to their clients and constituencies, and yet to remain nonpartisan and financially independent so as not to be viewed as the instrument of any particular individual, family or political party. Contrary to widespread perceptions of Islamic scholars and Islamic activists as being locked in perpetual conflict, the Muslim Brothers attracted a significant following among religious scholars (and not just the lower echelons), at least in the early years. Hasan al-Banna himself adopted an ambivalent stance vis-à-vis Islamic scholars in general and the Azharites in particular, but this did not prevent religious scholars from joining the Muslim Brotherhood or cooperating with it on specific issues. Several Azharites participated in the first General Guidance Office constituted in 1933, and *'ulama'* played an important role at the provincial level, though most of them later left or were expelled. Beyond their common interest in Islam, religious scholars and the Ikhwan also shared their hostility to communism or what they perceived as such.

RECRUITMENT AND ACTIVITIES

The Muslim Brothers recruited mainly through personal contacts, based on kinship, friendship and worship, and mosques and schools were their principal recruiting grounds. The transfer of government employees, teachers and Azhar officials helped to spread the message, to attract new adherents and to establish new branches. Hasan al-Banna's friend Shaykh Hamid 'Askariyya is a good example: appointed preacher (*wa'iz*) of the Suez Canal Zone by al-Azhar around 1930, he was shortly after transferred to Shubrakhit, in the Delta. The transfer turned out to be a blessing in disguise, for he formed a new Muslim Brother group there. In some areas, young members went out on Friday tours to proselytize among those whom they identified as practising Muslims. Hasan al-Banna himself was an untiring worker for the cause. He advocated a gradual approach that would make entry easy and demanded a full commitment only after a certain period of training. No rupture was required, just a regulation of behaviour – and the belief in obedience, struggle and sacrifice. In his *Memoirs*, al-Banna quotes Muhammad Sa'id al-'Urfi, a scholar and a Sufi and a former deputy in the Syrian parliament, who had been exiled by the French, who gave him the following advice when he visited Egypt in 1930 (*Memoirs*, p. 98):

> Do not refrain from accepting into the *da'wa* those who come short of fulfilling all their duties towards God and still commit some minor misdeeds (*ma'asi*) as long as you know that they are God-fearing, disciplined and obedient. They will soon repent. The Islamic call is like a hospital with a doctor who offers treatment, and a patient who seeks

> such treatment. Do not close the door in their face. If you can attract them by any means, do it, for this is the prime task of the Islamic call.

However, al-'Urfi also warned him not to accept those who were going to corrupt the community though they prayed and fasted. In later years, a Muslim Brother was to describe the "open door policy" in the following way (quoted from Lia, *Society*, p. 162):

> We, the Brotherhood, are like an immense hall that can be entered by any Muslim from any door to partake of whatsoever he wishes. Should he seek Sufism, he shall find it. Should he seek comprehension of Islamic jurisprudence, he shall find it. Should he seek sports and scouting, it is there. Should he seek battle and armed struggle, he shall find it.

After al-Banna's transfer to Cairo, he started to make what became known as "round tours" through Egypt, which proved to be an important element in creating a sense of belonging among members. These tours principally served to reinforce existing groups or branches, but of course they also exposed members, and Hasan al-Banna in particular, to realities on the ground, notably in the Upper Egyptian countryside. Everything was carefully planned and members of their youth section were deployed wherever they existed, creating an image of strength and order. Al-Banna made special efforts to court local notables and opinion makers, visiting mosques and private homes. Police and other government officials were invited to meetings to win their approval. Still, distrust could not be altogether eliminated, for the Ikhwan declared it their aim to fight prostitution, alcohol and other abominations, which the authorities were prepared to tolerate.

Starting in the summer of 1936, the first "summer delegations" (*ba'tha sayfiyya*) of student members were formed, which were later enlarged to include civil servants and religious scholars, to tour the countryside in imitation of al-Banna's circuits – and the *hijra* of the Prophet. A special tract was written for them, and they also received a certificate. Young preachers, especially preachers not sent out by al-Azhar, were still a novelty at the time. Initially, it was not easy to find volunteers who were prepared to tour the countryside in the hottest months of the year. By 1939, the tours had become routine and a new administrative body was created, headed by al-Banna himself. In addition to the Qur'an, the life of the Prophet, and basic elements of Islamic law and history, al-Banna's *Risalat al-Jihad* was required reading for these teams.

In the early 1930s, the Muslim Brother press did not play a significant role in spreading the call – quite in contrast to the well-known dictum that whoever wished to set up a political party in Egypt started by publishing a journal. The activists of Arab cultural and religious awakening, *al-nahda* and Salafiyya, had equally relied on the press to make their opinions known to a broader public. As a result, Egypt's market for dailies and periodicals was crowded, and it was difficult to find an audience. Al-Banna's writings and the Muslim Brother publications in general were mostly addressed to those who were already members. In other words, they were mostly for internal consumption.[6]

The press effort began rather inauspiciously with a newsletter called *The Guide's Message* (*Risalat al-Murshid*), of which only two issues were published in December 1932 and January 1933. In June 1933, a weekly called *Jaridat al-Ikhwan al-Muslimin* (*JIM*) was launched with the support of Muhibb al-Din al-Khatib, whose publishing house printed it until the Muslim Brotherhood acquired its own printing press in June 1934. Until November 1937, Hasan al-Banna held the licence; its first editor-in-chief was Shaykh Tantawi Jawhari, a retired Dar al-'Ulum professor who also taught at Cairo University and the editor of a multi-volume Qur'an commentary called *Tafsir al-Jawahir*. In 1936–7, Hasan al-Banna's father acted as director; occasionally, his old teacher Shaykh Muhammad Zahran contributed an article. Like the Muslim Brotherhood as a whole, *JIM* saw much change in format and iconography, yet in contrast to the mother organization it remained hampered by insufficient funds, limited circulation and a small readership.

Membership figures are difficult to ascertain, largely because of the lack of verifiable data, combined with what has been called political arithmetic, that is, figures put forth for political ends, either to exaggerate the strength of the Ikhwan or to downplay their number.[7] So far, no membership rosters have been found that could shed light on the social composition of the leadership and rank and file. What we have are mostly statements from Muslim Brother sources, newspaper articles and reports of the Egyptian secret police held in British archives. Added to the problem of figures is the fact that membership was graded. For lack of other sources, the number of branches is usually taken as an indication of the size and scope of the organization. However, the branches varied considerably regarding their membership numbers, structure and quality. The unity of the movement and the degree of centralization with Hasan al-Banna firmly at the helm must not be overrated. Significantly, documents from the 1930s often refer to Jam'iyyat al-Ikhwan al-Muslimin in the plural. While Hasan al-Banna was definitely the head of the original Isma'iliyya group and later the Cairo branch, the Brothers in his native al-Mahmudiyya functioned as an extension of the local Hasafi Benevolent Society headed by Ahmad al-Sukkari, and those in Shubrakhit, founded by Hamid 'Askariyya, appear to have been equally autonomous.

At the time of the First General Conference, held in June 1933, the Society reportedly had a total fifteen branches: one in Cairo, five in the Suez Canal Zone and the remaining nine in the Delta. In the latter half of 1933, some twenty new branches were opened, some of them quite small. Leaflets distributed and posters attached to the walls of mosques and coffeehouses were reportedly unable to attract larger audiences, and lectures were sparsely attended. At the same time, the Society made its first appearance in Upper Egypt, or, to be more precise, in Asyut, in the home province of Sayyid Qutb. The Second General Conference in January 1934 was attended by seventy-six delegates from twenty-four branches; others were unable to send a delegate. By 1936, the total number of branches may have exceeded 100. In July 1936, the Society's newspaper estimated the number of branches to be 150, which were still heavily concentrated in the Delta. At about the same time, British intelligence estimated the total number of members to be about 800, though the total number of adherents may well have exceeded several thousand.

Finances were gradually improved, among other things by collecting a piastre from every member during Ramadan and on the Prophet's birthday. Even so, funding remained precarious, as membership fees were based on income and poor members were exempted. For the same reason, social and charitable work was still on a modest scale, involving mostly a number of Qur'anic schools and workshops designed to create some income for poor students. In 1933, a pharmacy was opened in Cairo, marking the beginning of Muslim Brother engagement in the health sector. Projects were financed through individual contributions and the alms "tax," *zakat*, supplemented by support from local notables and mosques. There is evidence that at least in late 1937, the Brotherhood also received government support channelled through municipal councils.[8]

Social and charitable work was closely linked to the fight against Christian missionaries from Europe and America, a long-standing concern in Muslim as well as Coptic circles. But this fight was also entangled in the power game, with dangerous repercussions for Muslim–Christian relations in the country.[9] In June 1933, the former (and future) Shaykh al-Azhar Mustafa al-Maraghi formed a Committee for the Defence of Islam, which Hasan al-Banna joined along with prominent members of the Liberal Constitutionalist Party, such as Muhammad Husayn Haykal, and a number of dissident Wafdists, who used the occasion to enhance their Islamic credentials. In addition, the Muslim Brothers decided to form special committees to combat the missionaries and sent an open letter to the king urging him to take appropriate action to stop their activities.

ENTERING THE POLITICAL STAGE: 1938–49

The Muslim Brothers did not get involved in regional affairs until the mid-1930s and they did not formally announce their ambition to play a role in national politics until 1938–9. The sequence of political engagement – first abroad, then at home – merits attention.

LOOKING BEYOND EGYPT

Hasan al-Banna's interest in the Hijaz and Yemen was originally not linked to his role in the Muslim Brotherhood, but to his father's scholarly work and efforts to recruit Egyptian teachers for the fledgling educational systems in the two countries. Already in 1928, Hasan al-Banna had considered moving to the Hijaz, which had recently been conquered by Ibn Sa'ud and attached to his expanding domain, to teach there for a number of years. The opportunity seemed to present itself again in 1932 when al-Banna was still in Isma'iliyya. After he had given a talk at the YMMA club in Cairo, a Yemeni dignitary approached him to discuss the spread of atheism and immorality (in Yemen!) that needed to be resisted. Would al-Banna consider coming to Yemen as a teacher? Again he said yes, and again the plan came to naught. In the autumn of 1934, contacts were established with Hijazi scholars visiting Cairo. The visitors took a lively interest in Ahmad al-Banna's work on Ahmad b. Hanbal's *Musnad*; the first volume of *al-Fath al-rabbani* had just been printed and its subject happily agreed with the Wahhabi doctrine of the kingdom, which had developed out of the Hanbali school of law (but note that copies were also sent to Yemen which was decidedly non-Wahhabi, with the ruling dynasty representing the Zaydi school of law and the majority of the population in the southern part of the country following the Shafi'i school).

Like other Muslim Arab activists, such as Rashid Rida and Muhibb al-Din al-Khatib, al-Banna admired Ibn Sa'ud and placed high hopes in him, even though this was not without domestic risks, given Egyptian interests in the caliphate (more on this below). In February 1936 Hasan al-Banna left with a group of Muslim Brothers for his first pilgrimage to Mecca and Medina. Over the following years he would try to go regularly, for religious as well as for political reasons, for the *hajj* was also the occasion to establish and maintain international ties. The Sa'udi contacts were cultivated over the following years. Yet contacts are not the same as allegiance or dependence, as was shown by the conflict over a critical article by a young Sa'udi author in a Muslim Brother periodical in May 1939 and Ibn Sa'ud's reluctance to allow local branches of the Ikhwan to form in his country.

The Arabian Peninsula played a certain role in the gradual spread of the Muslim Brothers' message beyond Egypt. But it was the campaign in favour of Arab Palestine that propelled them to prominence, attracting attention at home and abroad, even though they acted only as junior partners of the YMMA and a number of prominent "Islamic" personalities. As a benevolent society the Muslim Brothers were prohibited by law from engaging in politics. But they could not be barred from taking up the cause of Muslims at home and abroad, just as Christians or Jews could not be prevented from concerning themselves with their coreligionists in other parts of the world. Already in 1928, al-Banna had informed prominent Muslim personalities of the new organization he had founded. They included the mufti of Jerusalem, Hajj Amin al-Husayni. A small Muslim Brother delegation visited Syria and Palestine in 1935, made up of Hasan al-Banna's brother 'Abd al-Rahman al-Sa'ati and Muhammad As'ad al-Hakim.

They met Amin al-Husayni in Jerusalem and Islamic scholars and activists in Damascus.

Modest though it was in scope and impact, the visit led to contacts with the prestigious Makassed Philanthropic Islamic Association (Jam'iyyat al-Maqasid al-Khayriyya al-Islamiyya) in Beirut, founded in 1878, which asked the Muslim Brothers for an instructor. Significantly, it was the visit of a large delegation of this organization that came to Egypt in March 1936 (*before* the outbreak of the Arab Revolt in Palestine) that brought the Muslim Brothers to the attention of British intelligence, not their size or their press or other activities. Even so, a member of the Special Section of the ministry of interior remarked:

> I consider that the "Moslem Brethren Society" will in the course of time be in a position to produce a reckless and heedless generation who will not abstain from selling their lives cheap and whose best wish would be to die as martyrs for the sake of God and their country.

While it was "growing in strength," he believed, it was "not at present in any way dangerous."[1] In the 1930s, a number of "branches" emerged in other Arab countries, some of them founded by students returning from Cairo to their native countries, whose size and importance, however, should not be overestimated.

The Young Men's Muslim Association had become interested in Palestine since the disturbances at the Wailing Wall in August 1929. It also took the lead in rallying Muslim opinion in Egypt once the Arab Revolt started in April 1936. A Supreme Council for Relieving Palestinian Victims was created, which al-Banna and other Muslim Brothers joined.[2] Muslim Brother activities were wide-ranging, from individual acts of protest to mass rallies and fund-raising campaigns. The Muslim Brothers sent petitions to political and religious leaders at home and abroad. At the same time, they called for a boycott of Jewish business in Egypt, which they accused of collaborating with the Zionist enemy, acting as its Fifth Column in Egypt. Students on summer tours to the Egyptian countryside were charged with mobilizing support for Arab Palestine. Mass meetings were held, demonstrations staged, pamphlets printed and a publication of the Palestinian Higher Arab Committee entitled *War and Destruction in Palestine* (*al-Nar wa-l-dimar fi filastin*) distributed in large numbers. Anti-imperialist critique was still rare in the Society's press in the early 1930s when the Muslim Brothers attempted to avoid government attention, but it was openly voiced at closed meetings. Their activities earned the Muslim Brothers some respect, especially among nationalist youth. But they also produced negative effects: in July 1936 the police searched their headquarters and from then on kept a close eye on them, inaugurating a phase of increased government surveillance, if not harassment. Hasan al-Banna was briefly detained, but the British ambassador felt that putting him in prison would only benefit the Ikhwan. Fund-raising in favour of Palestine also fuelled charges of misappropriation of funds within the Muslim Brotherhood itself. More importantly, the Palestine campaign contributed to a growing radicalization among its rank and file.

GOING POLITICAL AT HOME

The mid-1930s were a time of transition, when Egypt was moving from a political system based on patron–client relationships to a system shaped by ideological parties and mass mobilization, at least in the cities. Egypt was still ruled by large landowners and a local bourgeoisie of foreign and Egyptian background, and political decisions were largely monopolized by what has been called the "triangle" of the British, the palace and the Wafd. But their rule no longer went unchallenged. Al-Banna and the Muslim Brotherhood at large continued to cast themselves in the role of counsellors, offering guidance to the leaders of the country and the Muslim community, enjoining good, and if necessary prohibiting wrong. The highest body of the Society was significantly called Maktab al-Irshad al-'Amm, the General Guidance Office. Given their vision of Islam as a comprehensive "system" (*nizam*) regulating individual life and public affairs, this included politics. The very impulse that had led to the foundation of the Muslim Brotherhood reflected political concerns; their commitment to Islamic morality and education could not but touch on politics. Yet to address issues commonly perceived as political is not the same as assuming the role of political opposition. In a series of editorials in *Jaridat al-Ikhwan al-Muslimin* that started in April 1934 and was later published as the tract *To What Do We Summon People?*, Hasan al-Banna declared:[3]

> O our people: With the Qur'an in our right hand and the Sunna in our left, and with the deeds of the pious ancestors among the sons of this nation as our example, we call on you. We summon you to Islam, the teachings of Islam, the laws of Islam, and the guidance of Islam, and if this is politics for you, then it is our policy. And if the one summoning you to these principles [Islam] is a politician, then, God be praised, we are the most deeply rooted of men in politics ... Let not words conceal the facts for you, and names objectives, and objectives essentials: Islam does have a policy embracing happiness in this world and salvation in the thereafter.

In spring 1938, Hasan al-Banna announced a new phase of formation (*takwin*) or "special call" (*al-da'wa al-khassa*), that is to say, a call directed at select cadres of the Society only. At the same time, he declared the Muslim Brothers' intention to enter the political arena and to address political issues openly. In a passionate speech before the Society's Student Section, he insisted on the comprehensive nature of Islam that allowed for no distinctions between religion and politics (*Ila l-tullab*, p. 8):

> Tell me, Brothers: if Islam is something other than politics, society, economy and culture, what is it then? Is it only prostrations devoid of a pulsating heart? ... Did the Qur'an reveal a perfect, fixed and detailed system just for that? ... It is precisely to such a weak and narrow understanding of Islam that the enemies of Islam try to confine the Muslims so that they can mock them and say to them, "We left you your freedom of religion."

To the outside world he declared (quoted from Lia, *Society*, p. 206):

> Islam is worship and leadership, religion and state, spirituality and action, prayer and *jihad*, obedience and government, the book and the sword. None of these can be separated. God will subdue with might what cannot be subdued through the Qur'an ... The time for action has come, Brothers ... We will move from the general call to the special call and from a call based on words (alone) to one based on words accompanied by struggle and action. We will direct our call to the leaders of the country: its notables, ministers, rulers, elders, delegates and political parties and invite them to follow our method. We will place our programme in their hands and demand that they lead this Muslim country, the leader of the Islamic world, on the path of Islam with courage and without hesitation ... If they respond to our call and adopt the path to this goal, we will support them. But if they resort to duplicity or evasion and hide behind false excuses and arguments, then we are at war with every leader, party chief or organization that does not work to support Islam and does not move to restore the rule and glory of Islam.

This was an open challenge, if not a threat, and it provides a glimpse of al-Banna's concept of politics and the Ikhwan's mission: there was only one legitimate path, the path of Islam, and the Muslim Brothers stood for it; dissent could not be based on any legitimate alternative view, but only on illegitimate devices and desires. Some of the members took his call to wage war literally and in June 1938 clashed with the police, leading to arrests. Al-Banna was alarmed and dismissed the radicals from all leadership positions. As a result, a group of activists known as The Youth of Our Lord Muhammad (Shabab Sayyidna Muhammad) formed or came to the fore and this eventually split off from the mother organization. At the Fifth General Conference held in January 1939, al-Banna confirmed that the Muslim Brotherhood had entered its political phase, without, however, presenting a detailed programme and agenda to his audience.

What the Muslim Brothers propagated was essentially the ideal of national unity combined with the denunciation of party politics or factionalism (*al-hizbiyya*) as harmful and divisive. Considering the fact that the interwar period has often been called the age of party politics in Egypt, this was not a minor point. Yet the Muslim Brothers were not the only ones to criticize "partyism" and partisanship. Already in the 1920s, Sa'd Zaghlul, the leader of the Wafd, had frequently done so, claiming for the Wafd the role of representative of the nation at large; by the 1930s, the critique had become commonplace. Many Egyptians subscribed to the ideal of one nation undivided. What the Muslim Brothers had to offer was patriotic loyalty recast in Islamic terms, with a shift of focus from the Egyptian nation to the Muslim community, *umma*, without sacrificing one to the other. In 1938, the Ikhwan sent an open letter to the king and leading politicians, which was later published under the title *To the Light* (*Nahwa l-nur*), urging them to dissolve all parties and to create a unified front – a call that, under the circumstances, could be interpreted as directed primarily against the Wafd.

Apart from the Palestine campaign, the Muslim Brothers' main instruments of political action were still words. In May 1938, a new weekly called *The Warner* (*al-Nadhir*) announced its political character by calling itself "an Islamic political weekly based on the principles of the Muslim Brothers."[4] Its emblem showed the two crossed swords with the Qur'an that would serve as the official symbol of the Muslim Brotherhood. To avoid problems with the authorities, the licence required for journals and newspapers under Egyptian law was held by a lawyer, and Salih 'Ashmawi (1910–83) was its editor-in-chief. *Al-Nadhir* had a wider circulation than *Jaridat al-Ikhwan al-Muslimin*, which had closed a little earlier, although it still targeted members rather than a wider public.

But Hasan al-Banna did not give himself up to politics entirely. In 1939, he acquired the licence to continue *al-Manar*, which had suffered a decline after the death of Rashid Rida in July 1935.[5] This was no small achievement, considering that *al-Manar* was a serious journal with scholarly contributions and that al-Banna was neither a scholar nor a professional journalist. By his own account, the Rida family invited him to take over the journal. He hesitated: it was a great honour but also a heavy burden and a difficult task, he had no time, and the government had already closed down two of the Ikhwan's periodicals. Eventually he gave in. Shaykh al-Azhar Mustafa al-Maraghi wrote the preface for the first issue edited by al-Banna. Between July 1939 and September 1940 six issues appeared; then *al-Manar* was shut down by the government, this time for good. Al-Banna started his own contribution with a commentary on Sura 13 with its famous reference to self-help (see below), and also published several fatwas in *al-Manar*. The fact that his contributions should be classified as fatwas (rather than, say, answers to legal questions, *masa'il fiqhiyya*) indicates that the term was used loosely, departing from the strict rules of the genre.

PREPARING FOR *JIHAD*: ROVERS AND BATTALIONS

In Egypt, as in many countries of Europe and the Middle East, the 1930s witnessed the spread of boy scouting and paramilitary youth organizations, and the Muslim Brothers were part of this broader phenomenon. All these organizations took as their founding principle the well-known Roman maxim of *mens sana in corpore sano*, "a healthy spirit in a healthy body," and the idea that outdoor sports could serve as a useful outlet for young men in the difficult years of adolescence. The emphasis on physical exercise combined with spirituality, involving disciplining the body, mind and soul, were also reminiscent of East Asian martial arts. In the Middle East, the military idiom was not the speciality of "extremists" like Young Egypt, and it was not limited to Muslim Arabs. The Zionist youth movement, with its emphasis on ideological and physical training, followed the same pattern, shirts included: the Revisionist Brith Trumpeldor (Betar) is a case in point.

In Egypt, the Wafd recruited Youth Committees (Lijan al-Shabab) and trained them on the basis of the principles of loyalty, obedience, order and self-sacrifice.[6] In December 1935 it set up paramilitary Blue Shirt Groups (Firaq al-Qumsan al-Zarqa') to defend the party against its rivals. Although headed by the Copt Makram 'Ubayd, the Blue Shirts had recourse to an Islamic vocabulary: their ranks were called *fityan* (young men, evoking the ideal of chivalrous manliness, *futuwwa*), *ansar* (after the Medinese "helpers" of the Prophet), and *mujahids* (those engaged in *jihad*). By late 1937, membership was estimated at about 30,000, with some overlap with the Wafdist Youth Committees. A competing student group recruited from among the Liberal Constitutionalist and the National parties was also run on paramilitary lines, again with uniforms and badges. The years 1936 and 1937 saw repeated clashes between Young Egypt's Green Shirts and the Wafdist Blue Shirts, as well as acts of violence directed against Egyptian political leaders.

Hasan al-Banna was aware of contemporary developments in Europe, including the rise of fascism, and yet the buildup of uniformed units cannot be attributed solely to fascist influences. The Muslim Brothers had already set up Excursion Groups (Firaq al-Rahhala) in Isma'iliyya in the early 1930s.[7] In the mid-1930s they were renamed Rover Scouts (Jawwala) and patterned more consciously on the Egyptian Boy Scouts (Jam'iyyat al-Kishafa al-Ahliyya), the Young Men's Muslim Association and paramilitary movements inspired by contemporary European models. The Rovers offered healthy outdoor activities, companionship and excitement in the spirit of Egyptian patriotism and Islamic sentiment, which proved more attractive to young men than preaching in remote villages in the middle of August. Until a professional instructor was found, they were trained by al-Banna himself.

Some traits distinguished the Rovers from their more overtly secular counterparts: in addition to a specific kind of instruction or indoctrination, including frequent reference to the hero-warriors of the early Islamic period, prayer and night vigils constituted an important element of their training. The Rovers thus drew on a variety of repertories, Islamic as well as European: the spirit of *jihad* was constantly invoked; the *futuwwa* movement best known from the 'Abbasid era, with its emphasis on chivalrous masculinity, brotherhood and mutual help provided a historical antecedent, and Sufi practices of self-discipline were consciously employed. Communal devotions included the prayers and blessings taken from al-Banna's tract *Risalat al-Ma'thurat*, dated 1355/1936–7, which he explicitly defined as a *wird* and *wazifa*, as known from the Sufi tradition.

In 1938 the Rovers were formally registered with the Egyptian National Boy Scout Association, protecting them when all paramilitary units were dissolved in the wake of clashes between Green Shirts and Blue Shirts, and giving them access to economic benefits. By that time they were headed by Mahmud Labib, a retired army officer and former member of the National Party (al-Hizb al-Watani), who in 1911 had fought against the Italians in Libya, spent several years in Turkey and Germany and was later to become a major figure in the Brotherhood's Special Apparatus. In addition to providing order and security at public events the Rovers also engaged in social work and emergency help, becoming the most popular "face" of the Ikhwan alongside Hasan al-Banna himself. It is important to note that in the interwar period the Rovers do not seem to have been involved in any violence and that they operated entirely in the open. Still, the military idiom, drills and exercises must have left their imprint on the minds of the young men enrolled in them.

Already in the autumn of 1937, Battalions (*kata'ib*) were created for "initiated" members, who were recruited from the ranks of the Rovers.[8] Their creation coincided with the Arab Revolt in Palestine but predated the political phase formally announced in 1938–9. Each Battalion comprised ten to forty members, who had to give a special oath (*bay'a*) of commitment to "action, obedience and secrecy." A special programme combined ideological instruction and military training during the day with nightly vigils of *dhikr* and prayer patterned on the example of the Prophet and explicitly associated with Sufi practices. Members were required to study two confidential tracts, *On Method* (*Risalat al-Minhaj*), written by al-Banna in the spring of 1938, and *Instructions* (*Risalat al-Ta'alim*), written during the summer camp in 1938 to replace the former; it was later taught to the rank and file as well. Although considerable effort was devoted to mobilizing cadres, the Battalions never came close to al-Banna's expectations, who had originally hoped to recruit as many as 300 units with 12,000 members. At the same time, the Rovers grew from a few hundred members in 1935 to several thousand in 1941.

PATRONS WITHOUT CLIENTS? THE MUSLIM BROTHERS, THE PALACE AND PARTY POLITICS

Relations with party politicians, the palace and the king were sensitive and disputed, in their own time as much as later. They were designed to gain recognition, seek goodwill, and preempt conflict, but also to avoid dependence. The result was considerable unease, with the uniting factors of common interests and enemies barely outweighing conflicts over class and moral issues. If one is to believe al-Banna and other leading Muslim Brothers, they were living in a different world from the party politicians. They were working for a higher goal: the regeneration of Islam was at stake, as was the salvation of Egypt, if not the world at large. Islam stood opposed to weakness and corruption, as did moral integrity to depravity. The Muslim Brothers were counsellors, offering guidance. They knew no personal interest. They did not seek power for themselves. They were by definition nonpartisan. Party politics were anathema to them. How, then, could they enter into tactical games with party politicians? And yet they did, or at least Hasan al-Banna and a handful of his closest confidants did. There can be no doubt that al-Banna was deeply critical of party politics and the ruling elite more generally, and so were the Ikhwan at large. Still, there was room for manoeuvre. Connections existed to the Liberal Constitutionalist Party, which was dominated by large landowners. Individual Muslim Brothers maintained good relations with Wafdists, especially in the provinces. Some had been Wafdists before joining the Brotherhood, and a number retained their Wafdist sympathies even after. Yet their privileged partners were the palace and politicians close to it.

Rumours about Muslim Brother ties to palace politicians threatened the carefully cultivated image of a movement above party politics, serving only God, Islam and the nation. These rumours were not unfounded: Hasan al-Banna did have links to the palace and palace politicians, and the rise of the Muslim Brothers entailed competition with the Wafd as the major mass movement in the country, even though in the 1930s the Ikhwan cannot possibly have been seen as equal to the Wafd, the latter's steady weakening notwithstanding. Through the Young Men's Muslim Association, al-Banna met Prince 'Umar Tusun, a prominent member of the Egyptian royal family and one of the chief patrons of the YMMA. In 1935–6, al-Banna established relations with 'Ali Mahir Pasha, a friend of the royal family and one of the most influential politicians of the interwar period, with a wide network of clients and associates, including 'Abd al-Rahman 'Azzam, 'Aziz 'Ali al-Misri and Muhammad Salih Harb (who had just assumed leadership of the YMMA), all of them close to the palace. 'Ali Mahir also cultivated ties with Islamic organizations, including Young Egypt and the Muslim Brothers.

Were there any ideological sympathies involved? Did "conservatism" serve as a common denominator? It would seem that more than a broadly defined social and moral conservatism, which in any event was shared by broad sectors of the Egyptian populace, it was anti-communism that provided the common ground between the Muslim Brothers and their political allies. This applies even to the Wafd: if to its liberal wing the Muslim Brothers were always anathema, the so-called right wing led by Fu'ad Siraj al-Din Pasha saw them as useful allies against communism. It is all the more ironic that al-Banna and some of his associates should at times have been suspected of communist leanings. What these suspicions indicate above all is the inability of observers, local as well as foreign, to fully grasp the socio-cultural vision and mission of the Muslim Brothers.

There is no indication that Hasan al-Banna was opposed to the monarchy, or the person of the king, be it King Fu'ad (r. 1917–36), the youngest son of Khedive Isma'il, or his son Faruq. In his writings, al-Banna strikes a respectful if not reverential note, with his critique of royal conduct carefully guarded. Relations with the king have to be seen in the wider context of Turkey's abolition of the caliphate in 1924, the movement to restore the caliphate, the king's ambitions to be appointed caliph and, last but not least, the critique of party politics.[9] Three men played a crucial role in this context: the king himself, 'Ali Mahir Pasha and Shaykh al-Azhar Mustafa al-Maraghi. Prince Faruq was proclaimed king upon his father's death on 28 April 1936, when he was still a minor. These were critical times: the Anglo-Egyptian Treaty of Alliance signed in August 1936 enhanced Egypt's formal independence without satisfying nationalist demands for full independence, which would have included the withdrawal of all British military forces from the country; the Muslim Brothers were openly hostile to the treaty.

Faruq was crowned king upon coming of age in July 1937 and was studiously portrayed as "the righteous king," *al-malik al-salih*; some of his supporters went so far as to acclaim him publicly as commander of the faithful, *amir al-mu'minin*, though he himself was careful not to lay claim to the caliphal title, or, as a British diplomat put it, to pursue the caliphate grail. The Wafd strongly opposed all moves to promote Faruq as a religious figure: for them, there was to be "no politics in religion." The palace in turn tried to discredit the Wafd as a Coptic clique, a not-so-hidden criticism of the prominent role of Copts in Wafdist ranks, including one of their most prominent leaders, (William) Makram 'Ubayd.

In marked contrast to the Wafd, the Muslim Brothers demonstrated their loyalty to the throne and paid Faruq homage, with the Rover Scouts on conspicuous display. When the editor-in-chief of *Jaridat al-Ikhwan al-Muslimin* attacked the royal show of piety, al-Banna distanced himself from him. Still, the Muslim Brothers maintained their self-appointed role as critical advisers to the high and mighty:

> The king is the legitimate ruler of this country ... The position of the Muslim Brothers towards the Palace is that of allegiance and love ... However, this does not prevent us from giving fair advice and uttering a word of truth if the General Guidance Council [sic] notices anything which makes this necessary.[10]

Note the moral idiom and the clear reference to traditional notions of giving advice and speaking up for truth. Note also the sense of righteousness with which the Muslim Brothers cast themselves in the role of moral arbiter. Moral opprobrium was frequently voiced in the Brotherhood press. Moral opprobrium, however, is not the same as opposition, let alone revolutionary designs. Hasan al-Banna remained loyal to the king to the very end.

Relations with al-Azhar were equally tied to larger issues. Both sides shared certain goals, but they were also competitors. The Muslim Brothers openly challenged al-Azhar's claim to be the voice of (Sunni) Islam, and many Muslim Brothers including al-Banna himself censured al-Azhar's lack of zeal and social impact. A younger generation of Muslim Brothers, represented notably by Shaykh Muhammad al-Ghazali (1917–96), himself an Azhar graduate, would later denounce its outdated ("mediaeval") teaching methods and claim that al-Azhar had sold out to the rich and powerful to protect the interests of the religious class.

Al-Banna's critique of the institution was tempered by his good relations with Shaykh Mustafa al-Maraghi (1881–1945), whose pragmatic approach to socio-cultural reform he shared. Born in al-Maragha in the Upper Egyptian province of Suhaj, the son of an Azhar shaykh, an Azhar graduate and student of Muhammad ʿAbduh, al-Maraghi served for many years as chief Shariʿa judge of Sudan. He was regarded by many Azharites as an outsider, and too political a man altogether, when he was first appointed Shaykh al-Azhar in May 1928, only to resign in October 1929 over resistance to his reform plans and opposition from the palace. Al-Maraghi was close to the Liberal Constitutionalist Party, whose president re-installed him as Shaykh al-Azhar, against strong resistance from King Fu'ad, when he became prime minister in 1935. (Shaykh) Ahmad Hasan al-Baquri, who had joined the Muslim Brothers in the early 1930s and shortly after became the leader of al-Azhar's student union, helped to mobilize student support for al-Maraghi. From this time on, al-Maraghi also acted as religious adviser to Crown Prince Faruq.

Al-Banna first established contact with al-Maraghi in 1933, when the latter launched his campaign to fight Christian missionary activities, leading to a lasting friendship between the two men. Having attracted significant numbers of *'ulama'* in the early 1930s (who were not all Azharites), the Muslim Brothers made successful inroads among Azhar students in the late 1930s and early 1940s. By 1940 several of al-Azhar's Religious Institutes had developed into strongholds of the Muslim Brothers, without, however, eliminating the element of ambivalence and mutual suspicion.

THE SECOND WORLD WAR AND ITS AFTERMATH

When Britain declared war on the Axis powers in September 1939, Egypt refused to follow suit and merely broke off diplomatic relations with Germany. Still, the War imposed its conditions on the country: the government declared martial law, imposed censorship, and arrested several prominent politicians who were suspected of harbouring anti-British or pro-Axis feelings. The Muslim Brothers, being registered as a benevolent society and not a political party, benefited from a situation that impeded their rivals' movements, and expanded their social, educational and charitable work. The favourable situation did not prevent them from casting themselves in the role of perennial victim of government harassment, variously described as *mihna* and *fitna*. To explain the policy of restraint to their restive members, the leadership referred to the truce of Hudaybiyya, which the Prophet Muhammad had concluded with his Meccan enemies in 6/628, in order to build up sufficient strength to ultimately prevail over them. The leadership also insisted on the duty to obey orders.

The added weight the Brotherhood assumed through its flurry of activity and broadening social base attracted attention, so that it was now increasingly courted by politicians rather than it having to court them. Hasan al-Banna and a few other leading Muslim Brothers, first and foremost Ahmad al-Sukkari, continued to meet with individual politicians, groups and parties, and even with the British. There was nothing exceptional in these dealings, which were the stock of politics as played in Egypt under the monarchy. The only exceptional feature was that the Muslim Brothers claimed not to be doing what they were, in fact, doing – playing the political game. 'Ali Mahir continued to protect them even after the collapse of his government in mid-1940, as he was still in control of the Special Branch of Egyptian police, and provided financial support. Although 'Ali Mahir and other politicians acted as a patron towards the Muslim Brothers, at least for a time, the Brothers did not consistently play the part of faithful client.

In June 1940, Italy entered the War, declared its intention to oust the British from Egypt while fully respecting Egyptian sovereignty and bombed Egyptian territory; in retaliation, Cairo broke off relations with Rome. In spite of the tense situation, in January 1941 the Muslim Brothers held their Sixth General Conference in Cairo, which was attended by several thousand participants, with vocal calls for the termination of foreign interference and the nationalization of the Suez Canal. A month later, in late February 1941, Hasan al-Banna was transferred to a school in remote Qena, causing considerable alarm among the Brothers.[11] According to Muhammad Husayn Haykal, then minister of education and al-Banna's superior, the British were concerned about pro-Axis feelings among Egyptian opinion makers and their influence over the masses. They informed Prime Minister Husayn Sirri that Shaykh (note the title!) Hasan al-Banna was working for the Italians and asked him to put a stop to it. Their suspicions were not entirely unfounded as far as the external link is concerned, though they may have been wrong about its precise nature. There is evidence that the Muslim Brothers had received subsidies from the *German* Legation in Cairo prior to October 1939; later Mahmud Labib was named as the person involved in these transactions. Some of this money apparently went into the Muslim Brother campaign for Palestine. No sums are given, and direct contacts probably ended once all non-Jewish German citizens resident in the country were interned and deported after the breaking off of diplomatic relations with the Reich.

The prime minister felt that transferring al-Banna to Upper Egypt on the grounds that he was engaging in politics, which was illegal for a government employee, would satisfy British demands. Normally, such a transfer could be made without further ado, and this happened all the time. But not in this case. Haykal was approached by members of parliament and asked to reconsider the order. Personally he did not care either way (and so he cannot have seen al-Banna as posing that much of a threat) but he was concerned that the prime minister's change of heart might actually encourage al-Banna and further boost the Ikhwan. By his own account, al-Banna himself did not hesitate to go to Qena: not only was he a model civil servant who would obey instructions, he also hoped to organize Muslim Brother activities in this part of the country. And he did. On one notable occasion the Muslim Brother branch in Qena invited the local Coptic community to a tea party, and a large number came, including the local bishop, dealing a blow to all those who charged the Muslim Brothers with instigating sectarian conflict, *fitna ta'ifiyya*. After about four months of exile, al-Banna was allowed to return to Cairo, at the end of June 1941.

In the meantime, in April 1941 a nationalist government led by Rashid 'Ali al-Kaylani and supported by the Iraqi military counting on Axis support, challenged British rule in Iraq, threatening repercussions across the wider Middle East. Rumour spread of an impending anti-British uprising in Egypt. In June 1941, 'Aziz 'Ali al-Misri (1878–1965), a hero of Ottoman resistance against the Italian occupation of Libya in 1911–12, participant in the Arab Revolt of 1916, former chief of staff of the Egyptian army and a pivotal figure in Egyptian anti-British circles, was caught when attempting to join the Axis forces advancing in the Western Desert, under the command of Field Marshal Rommel.[12] Ahmad al-Sukkari was briefly detained because of his association with al-Misri. In October 1941, al-Banna, together with other leading Muslim Brothers, was arrested, after giving a public speech attacking imperialism and calling for the application of Islamic law; the Brotherhood's press was shut down and its meetings were banned. The authorities were even more alarmed when petitions carrying some 11,000 signatures came in from all parts of the country demanding al-Banna's release. He and his associates were visited by a cabinet minister in prison, and released, against British wishes, in November 1941. Hasan al-Banna came out of prison quite shaken and with his cautious instincts reinforced. To cheer up his followers, he gave a series of talks, but he also made contact with the British embassy in Cairo. The episode was registered by the Muslim Brothers as another sign of their oppression.

The advance of Axis forces in the Western Desert, combined with poor harvests and food shortages, created a tense atmosphere in the country. When the government decided to break off diplomatic relations with Vichy France, students took to the streets on 1 February 1942, chanting "Advance Rommel." The British ambassador, Sir Miles Lampson (later Lord Killearn), "asked" the king to instal a Wafdist government, which was expected to be anti-Axis and to this extent also pro-British, and he followed this demand with an ultimatum on 4 February 1942. The king yielded and appointed a Wafdist government under Mustafa al-Nahhas Pasha. Many Egyptians felt that by agreeing to British demands to form a government, the Wafd had betrayed the nation. The Wafd announced new parliamentary elections to be held in March 1942. When the Muslim Brothers prepared to nominate candidates in a number of districts, with Hasan al-Banna standing for Isma'iliyya in the sensitive Suez Canal Zone, the prime minister threatened him with internment should he and his fellow Muslim Brothers not withdraw, thus blocking the Muslim Brotherhood's access to parliament – a nonpolitical welfare association, as it should be remembered.[13] At the same time al-Nahhas offered a deal, which al-Banna accepted: he agreed to withdraw from the electoral campaign and published an open letter in *al-Ahram* in support of the 1936 Anglo-Egyptian Treaty (which the General Guidance Office had sharply criticized) as well as the Wafdist government more generally. In return, al-Nahhas promised to impose restrictions on alcohol and prostitution and to facilitate the Muslim

Brotherhood's activities. The arrangement secured its continued expansion and reinvigorated its press.

In November 1942, the battle of al-ʻAlamayn stopped the Axis forces in the Western Desert, reducing the threat to the British position in Egypt and the Middle East. In January 1945, new parliamentary elections were held under the government of Ahmad Mahir, one of the so-called minority cabinets. Hasan al-Banna again stood for Ismaʻiliyya; five other Muslim Brothers ran in other districts. They all failed or were foiled by the government acting under strong British pressure. Prime Minister Ahmad Mahir was shot by a member of the Islamic National Party (formerly Young Egypt) on 24 February 1945, after announcing his intention to declare war on Germany and Japan, a proposal seen as toadying to the British. Al-Banna and several other Muslim Brothers were briefly detained, and strict surveillance was imposed on the Muslim Brotherhood. The new cabinet of Mahmud Fahmi al-Nuqrashi Pasha finally declared war on the Axis on 26 February 1945. Hasan al-Banna again approached the British embassy to reach some kind of agreement, which, according to their own account, the British refused. The government increased its pressure and transferred al-Banna from Cairo to a school beyond Giza, finally prompting him to resign his position as teacher of Arabic. In fact it is difficult to imagine that he had served as a teacher in the government service for all those years. Reporting on a meeting with al-Banna on 17 October 1945, the British oriental counsellor noted (quoted from Abdel Nasser, *Britain*, p. 61):

> some eighteen months ago, he had been at great pains to explain to me that the objectives of his society were religious, cultural and social. At recent meetings of the Ikhwan el-Muslimin he had come out with clearly political objectives. Hassan al-Banna replied that the religious objectives in Islam were inevitably at times political ... He then went on to repeat his old thesis, namely that the Moslem Brethren were our most useful allies in a society threatened with dissolution. They were the greatest barrier against communism and the strongest factor working for stabilization. Islam, while democratic, was a force of conservation.

POST-WAR GROWTH AND EXPANSION

In spite of all these difficulties, the Muslim Brothers emerged significantly strengthened from the Second World War. Wartime disturbances and mass unemployment following the withdrawal of Allied forces from Egypt undermined the credibility of liberal democracy *à l'égyptienne* and the political system at large. The Wafd was compromised by its wartime collaboration with the British; the king, who had lost his popularity, and the so-called minority parties, which had never had any popular base to speak of, relied more heavily on the British than ever. The Muslim Brothers' strength rested on three pillars that enabled them to survive and spread under adverse circumstances: the regular organization with its broadening mass base; the Rover Scouts, which had become the most effective paramilitary youth group in the country; and the newly created Special Apparatus. In the turmoil of the post-war years, the Muslim Brothers were able to portray themselves successfully as the voice of Egypt – resonating and powerful. The Rovers in particular were deployed in a conscious staging of power. Their chants and slogans became well known: "God is great and praise be to him" (*Allahu akbar lillah al-hamd*), and "God is our aim, the Prophet is our leader, the Qur'an is our constitution, *jihad* is our path, death in the path of God is our highest hope. God is great, God is great" (*Allah ghayatuna, al-rasul za'imuna, al-qur'an dusturuna, al-jihad sabiluna, al-mawt fi sabil allah asma amanina. Allahu akbar, allahu akbar*).

Over the years, the Society of the Muslim Brothers had experienced continuous restructuring from above, with efforts at centralization alternating with greater freedom given to local branches, reflecting a policy of trial and error rather than consistent planning and effective control. The gradual evolution of thought and organization is well reflected in Hasan al-Banna's *Memoirs* in which he frequently noted that he "took the opportunity" to make a specific decision. By the end of the Second World War, the Muslim Brotherhood looked very much like a nationalist mass party. Like the Wafd Party, or the Indian Congress Party, it claimed to represent the nation at large, and in light of this vision, internal dissent not only amounted to weakness; it was illegitimate. In the years preceding the War, attempts to create an Islamic Front in cooperation with other Islamic associations had met with some success, and a number of smaller groups merged with the Muslim Brotherhood. In a comprehensive reorganization and purge in November 1938, local notables were replaced by cadres appointed by the General Guidance Office (MIA), and the new office of local "guides" (*murshids*) was introduced. In 1941, a Constituent Assembly (al-Hay'a al-Ta'sisiyya) consisting of 100 delegates selected by the MIA was created to act as a new central consultative body, based on the Islamic principle of consultation, *shura*, to replace the General Consultative Council (Majlis al-Shura al-'Amm).

Only two years later, yet another structure was established on a national scale to provide better protection for local units against government repression: the "family system" (*nizam al-usar*) provided for a framework of indoctrination and action constructed on horizontal ties of solidarity among members of individual cells or "families," though it was tightly woven into a comprehensive chain of command with Hasan al-Banna at the top. The terminology combined references to kinship and family, military unit, Sufi brotherhood and the Muslim community at large. Key terms were "familiarity" (*ta'aruf*), "understanding" (*tafahum*), "solidarity and responsibility" (*takaful*), terms that reflect skilful use of Arabic grammar, in that this particular noun form emphasizes the notion of reciprocity (*mutual* understanding, *mutual* responsibility), enjoined so forcefully in the Qur'an. Members were subject to detailed regulations for everyday behaviour, as laid down in Hasan al-Banna's tract *Instructions* (*Risalat al-Ta'alim*), complete with prayers and devotions (*wazifa*, *wird*) for all occasions as specified in his *Risalat al-Ma'thurat*.

In April 1944, the Muslim Brothers reorganized their women's section, commonly known as the "Muslim Sisters."[14] Around 1945, they opened a girls' school in Cairo; other activities took place in Alexandria. In October 1947 they published their first pamphlet, *Muslim Woman* (*al-Mar'a al-muslima*), freely using the terms "revolt" and "revolution," *inqilab* and *thawra*, and calling for a revival of women's proper roles and rights in the framework of Islam. One of the first issues they took up was dress: they opted first for a black headscarf (*tarha*), but when this elicited unfavourable comments because in Egypt black was the colour of mourning – the days of the 'Abbasids, when black was the colour of the court and dynasty, had long since passed – they exchanged it for a white one. By 1948, the Muslim Sisters reportedly had fifty branches in Egypt with some 5,000 members, many of them relatively well educated. The figure was substantial considering the low rate of organized political activity among Egyptian women at the time, but it was little compared to the success the Ikhwan had among young men. The slow growth of the women's section was related to resistance on the part of those Muslim Brothers who held conventional views on female modesty (views Hasan al-Banna shared) as well as to the lack of interest among educated women and female students, who reportedly resented what they perceived as a "return to the age of the harem." Interviews revealed that the Ikhwan's message failed to stir their imagination.

Muslim Brother activities in the social and economic domains expanded significantly during and after the Second World War. In September 1945, new statutes were adopted (only to be amended over subsequent years) to respond to changes in the legal status of welfare associations prepared by the ministry of social affairs. As government subsidies could be granted only to benevolent societies and the Society of the Muslim Brothers had become openly political, it renamed itself the Muslim Brother Organization (Hay'at al-Ikhwan al-Muslimin) and established a separate Section of Welfare and Social Services (Qism al-Birr wa-l-Khidma al-Ijtima'iyya) to serve as the conduit for public funds. Under the premiership of Isma'il Sidqi (1946–7), the Muslim Brothers again benefited from government support. They were allowed to publish *Jaridat al-Ikhwan al-Muslimin* in a new format and to buy newsprint at official (as opposed to black market) rates; the Rovers were able to purchase uniforms at a discount and to use government camps and facilities for their training.

Building on their long-standing investment in public education and their advocacy of modern teaching methods, the Muslim

Brothers opened new schools and kindergartens. It helped that in 1946 one of their members, Hasan al-'Ashmawi, served as minister of education. In line with the reformist project of the Arab revival and the Salafiyya, the Muslim Brothers had always advocated modern science and technology. In November 1944, they established a medical section and opened a number of clinics and pharmacies. At the same time, the Rovers played a widely publicized role in fighting natural disasters, notably the malaria epidemic in Upper Egypt in 1942–3 which caused some 20,000 casualties, the floods of 1945 and the cholera epidemic of 1947. To provide employment for their members and attract a following among the working class, the Muslim Brothers also established a number of industrial enterprises, of which the Spinning and Weaving Company with its mill at Shubra al-Khayma, opened in 1947, was the most important. It was also the site of fierce conflict with trade union activists affiliated with the left-wing Wafdist Vanguard as well as Marxist and communist groups who accused the Muslim Brothers of fascist methods, strike-breaking and spying for the government, serving the interests of imperialism.

Membership figures of the Muslim Brotherhood are as difficult to establish as for the interwar period, and by and large for the same reasons – the lack of verifiable empirical data combined with partisan reports. Accordingly, estimates vary greatly.[15] Hasan al-Banna spoke of 20,000 Muslim Brothers in 1936, and 100,000 in February 1939. Estimates for 1944 range from 100,000 to 500,000 members and supporters. In the absence of reliable membership figures, the number of branches still serves as the best indicator of the Brotherhood's size and reach into Egyptian society. According to their own statistics, the number of branches rose from 100 at the beginning of 1936 to 150 in July 1936 and 217 in June 1937, though most branches were quite small. By June 1938, there were some 300 branches; a survey published in May 1940, after the secession of the Shabab Muhammad, gave the total number as 265. The number of branches reached 500 in January 1941. By 1944, it was estimated at 1,000–1,500. Progress was most marked in Upper Egypt, where the Muslim Brothers benefited from the lack of competition from other groups and organizations. The situation was different in Cairo and Alexandria because of the expanding network, or "civil society," of religious, cultural and political associations in those cities.

On the whole, the Society of the Muslim Brothers thus constituted a provincial urban movement, though one controlled from the capital, Cairo. Its social base remained as "popular" as before, attracting for the most part students, government employees, shopkeepers and traders, artisans and small landowners. There is evidence that it also appealed to urban workers. At the same time, it reached deeper into the expanding professional class. The Muslim Brothers enjoyed strong support among schoolteachers, whom al-Banna considered especially useful as they were dedicated and respected, and in addition had free time on their hands. Even before the Second World War, close relations were established with the Teachers' Syndicate, one of Egypt's largest professional unions with more than 25,000 members, which originally had been associated with the Wafd. There is less information available about developments at the provincial level.

THE SPECIAL APPARATUS

By the end of the Second World War, the Muslim Brothers had established a place for themselves in Egyptian politics and society. As intermittent government support serves to show, they were not consistently perceived as a threat to the established order. Yet there had always been doubts concerning al-Banna's designs and the Muslim Brothers' true objectives. An agenda they certainly had. Whether it was "hidden" depends on how one interprets the Special Apparatus – also known as the Secret Apparatus or Military Wing (*al-jihaz* or *al-tanzim al-khass, al-jihaz al-sirri*) – they set up in the shadow of the War. In spite of a growing body of literature that began appearing in the mid-1980s, including memoirs and confessions of former members, the Secret Apparatus kept its secrets well. Much is still disputed, from the date of its creation to the precise nature of its link to Hasan al-Banna. Richard Mitchell has argued that this uncertainty may be related to its "fluidity and informality of structure" (*Society*, p. 206), but it also mirrored conflicting assessments. It should be said that a clandestine section preparing for armed struggle was not a Brotherhood invention. There were known antecedents among political parties from the Hizb al-Watani to the Wafd. The secret apparatus set up by the Wafd in 1919–20 provoked similar questions to those later addressed to the Muslim Brothers, as the ties of this apparatus to the Wafdist leadership remained unclear and controversial.

It appears most likely that the Special Apparatus was formed in 1940, with the active participation of prominent Muslim Brothers, including Salih 'Ashmawi (who seems to have maintained contact with the breakaway Shabab Muhammad), and the Rover Scouts and Battalions more particularly.[16] Frustration over continued British interference in Egyptian politics, glaring social inequality and rampant corruption had created strong pressure from below. Competition with Young Egypt equally played a role. In the late 1930s, Young Egypt shifted to an Islamic rhetoric and in 1940 it renamed itself the Islamic National Party (al-Hizb al-Watani al-Islami). In what appears as an attempt to "out-Brotherhood the Brotherhood," its leader Ahmad Husayn now attacked sin and immorality, called for a return to Islamic law and declared that force and revolution were inevitable. The Muslim Brothers, by contrast, were instructed by their leaders to avoid open confrontation and demonstrate their adherence to the constitution. Young Egypt activists taunted them for their weakness.

It was in these troubled times that Hasan al-Banna wrote his tract *Between Yesterday and Today*, which was to become required reading for members (*Rasa'il*, pp. 142f.):

> I would like to avow to you frankly that your message is yet unknown to many people, and that the day they know it and recognize its purposes and objectives, it will encounter their fierce opposition and strong enmity. You will then be faced with many hardships and obstructions ... The usurpers will employ every means to oppose

> you and to extinguish the light of your call ... There can be no doubt that you will enter a phase of trials and tribulations, when you will be imprisoned, detained, banished and exiled. Your property will be confiscated, your operations suspended and your homes searched. Indeed, your period of trial may last long ... But God has promised you that after all this [suffering] he will help those who struggle and reward those who do good ... Are you resolved to be the helpers of God (*ansar allah*)?

Given subsequent events, the words assumed a prophetic quality, though the trials and tribulations of the great persecution, *mihna*, of the 1950s went well beyond what al-Banna could have envisaged. He continued in the same context (*Rasa'il*, p. 144):

> Brothers: you are not a welfare organization, nor a political party, nor a local association with limited objectives. Rather, you are a new spirit entering the heart of this nation to give it new life through the Qur'an. You are a new light dawning and scattering the darkness of materialism through knowing God. You are a strong voice arising to echo the message of the Prophet ... Without exaggeration, you should feel entitled to see yourselves as the carriers of the burden that all others have refused. When people say to you, "What is it you call to?," say we call to Islam, the message of Muhammad (May God bless and save him!): government is part of it, and freedom is one of its obligations. If people were to say to you, "This is politics!," say this is Islam and we do not recognize such distinctions. And if they say to you, "You are agents of revolution," say we are agents of truth and peace in which we believe and exalt. If you rise against us or stand in the path of our call, then we have permission from God to defend ourselves, and you are unjust rebels. If they say to you, "You are seeking the help of individuals and associations," say we believe in God alone and repudiate what we were associating with him (Qur'an 40:84). If they persist in their aggression, say to them peace be upon you, we have no desire for the ignorant (Qur'an 28:55).

This was vintage al-Banna. What he was saying to his followers as well as to the outside world was that force was entirely justified but that the Muslim Brothers would not use it – a statement undermined by the fact that at that very moment, they were creating a parallel secret apparatus to train an army of young men to realize their goals, by force if necessary. At the Fifth General Conference of the Muslim Brotherhood, in January 1939, al-Banna had clearly distanced himself from a revolutionary course.[17] But he was walking a narrow path between demands for action and the perceived need to reach some kind of accommodation with the authorities. Several clashes in the provinces testified to the riotous mood among the rank and file. Many Ikhwan opposed any rapprochement with the establishment and cooperation with party politicians more specifically. Internal pressure increased with the outbreak of the Second World War, promising as it did more favourable conditions for declaring complete independence from Britain. As a result, there was no lack of cadres who pushed for militant action against the actual policy of restraint practised by al-Banna in spite of some fierce rhetoric. Many members were attracted to what Brynjar Lia called the "mystique of secret and flamboyant action" (Lia, *Society*, pp. 178f.).

The growing body of literature written by former members as well as critical observers has done little to modify Mitchell's judgement that although "before 1948 few members indeed knew about the secret apparatus, those who did – and after 1948 this number included most of the articulate members – found few if any reasons to resist it. Thus while the secret apparatus had relatively few members, it had, as a concept, large if inarticulate support."[18] Ideologically it could draw on the ideas of *jihad* and sacrifice that had been propagated and indeed celebrated by al-Banna and the Muslim Brothers at large. External support for the buildup of a military apparatus must not be downplayed, but neither should it be overrated. The protection offered by the Egyptian police under 'Ali Mahir Pasha, who advocated military training for Egyptian students, facilitated its formation. Training was specially organized, with Hasan al-Banna's *Risalat al-Jihad* serving as the main text of indoctrination, and included instruction in the use of firearms. Caches of weapons, many of them left over from the War or purchased from arms dealers, were stored. The Special Apparatus set up its own intelligence service, which focused on British installations. However, its larger objectives remained unclear; the same applies to whether enrolled members were aware of such objectives. What is clear is that throughout the War, the apparatus did not take up armed struggle against the British, the Zionists or their own domestic enemies.

Among the most controversial issues is the relationship between, on one side, the Special Apparatus, the Society of the Muslim Brothers and Hasan al-Banna, and, on the other, the Free Officers.[19] Again, individual contacts have to be distinguished from institutional ties. In the 1940s, contacts between the Muslim Brothers and what later became known as the Free Officers were limited to a small group of people: in addition to Hasan al-Banna, they included Anwar al-Sadat, ‘Abd al-Mun‘im ‘Abd al-Ra’uf, Kamal al-Din Husayn and, to a lesser extent, Jamal ‘Abd al-Nasir (Nasser). Al-Banna had first met Anwar al-Sadat in 1940 and again in 1942, when Sadat discovered that the Muslim Brothers had secretly started collecting arms though he felt that al-Banna could not be relied upon to offer the Free Officers actual support; as a result, a "tone of suspicion" developed between the two men. From August 1942, ‘Abd al-Ra’uf served as chief liaison between the officers and al-Banna. In 1944 al-Banna and Nasser met for the first time. There is no indication, however, of any concerted action or even plan of action.

Hasan al-Banna was not identical with the Society of the Muslim Brothers, which had long since outgrown its modest beginnings. Growth and diversification inevitably curtailed control from the top. Loyalty to al-Banna alone could not guarantee internal cohesion, and he was unable to supervise the membership to the extent he may have been able to at an earlier stage. In May 1946, internal dissent further weakened centralized control and strengthened the Special Apparatus: several Muslim Brothers accused ‘Abd al-Hakim ‘Abidin, the young secretary general of the Muslim Brotherhood, who was just about to marry Hasan al-Banna's sister Fatima (who for obvious reasons other Brothers had coveted too), of immoral conduct.[20] A committee of investigation acquitted ‘Abidin without, however, resolving the tension. One of al-Banna's deputies resigned in protest in April 1947, followed in late November 1947 by the expulsion of Ahmad al-Sukkari from the Society of the Muslim Brothers. This was serious, for al-Sukkari, who in 1938 had moved to Cairo to act as al-Banna's deputy (*wakil 'amm*), was not only al-Banna's boyhood friend; he was also widely perceived as the political thinker of the Brotherhood. It was al-Sukkari who served as the main liaison with 'Ali Mahir, Fu'ad Siraj al-Din and other politicians and as a result became the chief object of criticism for all those who objected to such contacts. It was even said that he saw himself as the political leader of the Ikhwan with al-Banna merely acting as their spiritual guide.

In a direct confrontation between the two men, however, al-Sukkari stood no chance. Like all previous critics and opponents, he had to go. Both men made their grievances public in open letters to the Egyptian press: al-Sukkari accused al-Banna of dictatorship and a dangerous complicity with anti-Wafdist forces, creating a situation in which the public considered the Muslim Brothers a "commodity to be bought and sold," whereas al-Banna reproached al-Sukkari for obfuscation and pinned responsibility for the Brotherhood's perceived political entanglement on him. As Sukkari's replacement, al-Banna chose none other than the acting head of the Special Apparatus, Salih 'Ashmawi. Leadership of the Special Apparatus passed on to the ambitious 'Abd al-Rahman al-Sanadi, a minor official in the ministry of agriculture.

BREAKDOWN: 1948–9

After the Second World War, social conflict and political discord, coinciding with the escalating crisis in Palestine, resulted in a breakdown of security in the country. Beginning in 1945 a series of assassinations had been carried out in Egypt by radical nationalists. In May 1945, two cinemas were bombed, presumably by militant Wafdists, with Egyptian lives lost, not foreign ones, although foreigners were the presumed target. The Special Apparatus made its first attacks on British installations as well as government offices and officials, while the Muslim Brothers and other nationalist forces stepped up their campaign against local Jews as the alleged Fifth Column of the Zionists in Palestine. At the same time, tension between Muslims and Copts was mounting. On 2 November 1945 ("Balfour Day"), Jewish and Christian property was looted in Cairo. In the autumn, labour strikes erupted at the large textile works in the Cairo suburb of Shubra al-Khayma. Uniformed units of Young Egypt, the Wafd and the Ikhwan paraded in public, flaunting their arms and explosives. Wafdists, Marxists and Muslim Brothers engaged in open fighting, and the former two spoke of the fascist terror committed by the latter.

Nationalists demanded that no negotiations be held with the British before the evacuation of all British military forces from Egypt and the Sudan. Al-Banna called on the country's leaders to prepare the nation for *jihad* and to boycott the British at all levels. Student unrest culminated in February and March 1946; some fifty students were killed in violent confrontations with British forces in Cairo and Alexandria. Treaty negotiations with the British were to resume in April 1946, and Prime Minister Isma'il Sidqi went to London in October of that year. After his return, violent protest broke out culminating in the Cairo riots of 25 November 1946. The authorities made widespread arrests across all political camps, including the Muslim Brothers. Hasan al-Banna himself was away on the pilgrimage. Isma'il Sidqi resigned as prime minister, and his successor, Muhammad Fahmi al-Nuqrashi Pasha, decided to take Egypt's case for complete independence to the United Nations.

Hasan al-Banna continued to give out conflicting signals to his followers. In *Friday Talks* published in spring 1947 in *Jaridat al-Ikhwan al-Muslimin*, he declared that there was only *jihad* and fight and struggle on the path of truth – and yet the Muslim Brothers needed to be patient in the face of the current *mihna* for battle was near, and it was not to be a battle between ordinary men but was the battle of the Qur'an. Only those who prohibited wrong could hope to survive impending punishment.[21] Meanwhile, the British military started their retreat from Cairo but remained firmly entrenched in the Suez Canal Zone. While the Security Council ignored the Egyptian case, it decided on 29 November 1947 to partition Palestine between Jews and Arabs.

In mid-February 1948 public attention briefly shifted to Yemen, where the assassination of Imam Yahya Hamid al-Din acted as a trigger for the so-called Constitutional Revolution, of which the Free Yemeni Movement was a major component.[22] There were rumours of Muslim Brother involvement in the events. The Muslim Brothers had indeed recruited among Yemeni students at al-Azhar and made contact with Yemeni personalities residing in Cairo or visiting the country; in the early 1940s, they established ties with members of the Free Yemeni Movement. Crown Prince Ahmad b. Yahya, however, defeated his rivals in March 1948 and succeeded his father as *imam*.

If the Muslim Brothers' role in the Yemen was controversial, though it cannot have been substantial, there was no doubt about the involvement of two members of the Special Apparatus in the assassination, in March 1948, of Ahmad al-Khazindar, a judge who had sentenced a Muslim Brother for throwing bombs at an Alexandria club. The murder was reportedly committed without al-Banna's knowledge and authorization, and he hastened to condemn it.[23] Several assassination attempts on Nahhas Pasha were allegedly made by members of the Sa'dist Party, which had split off from the Wafd.

At the same time, the Muslim Brothers were actively involved in the fighting prior to and immediately following the foundation of the State of Israel on 15 May 1948, having already rendered "technical assistance" to the Palestinians in the previous weeks and months (Mitchell, *Society*, pp. 56–8). In spring 1946, Hajj Amin al-Husayni, the former mufti of Jerusalem who had fled Palestine in 1937, arrived in Cairo. He had spent the years 1941–5 in Germany and territories occupied by it, openly collaborating with the Nazi regime; still, he retained his popularity among the Muslim Brothers and Arab nationalists, who called on the king to grant him asylum. Al-Banna joined his old friend 'Abd al-Rahman 'Azzam, head of the Arab League, created in March 1945, as well as 'Ali Mahir, Salih Harb and

'Ali 'Aluba, to form a Nile Valley Committee for the Defence of Palestine, to collect money and arms for the Palestinians. In October 1947, al-Banna ordered the Muslim Brothers to prepare for military *jihad* against the Zionist enemy, and a number of Ikhwan underwent military training. It is important to note that this was not clandestine work and that it was not perceived as a move against the Egyptian government, which actually permitted the training of volunteers if carried out by military officers. Some of these instructors were members of the Free Officers group or were later to become members. Anwar al-Sadat records meetings between al-Banna and a number of Free Officers, including Nasser, to discuss how best to unite their efforts.

In March 1948, the first detachment of Muslim Brother volunteers left for al-'Arish in the Sinai to enter a training camp in Syria. First encounters with Jewish units in the Negev ended in losses; at home the fallen volunteers were celebrated as martyrs. In spite of their enthusiasm, the volunteers' contribution to the fighting was limited, not least because of poor coordination among the Arab contingents sent to Palestine; the Jordanians in particular were deeply suspicious of Egyptian designs and curtailed their freedom of movement. The Muslim Brothers did, however, assist the Egyptian troops caught at Faluja near Gaza in October 1948, whom the Nuqrashi government refused to relieve and of whom Nasser was to become the most famous member. Some volunteers subsequently moved to the Suez Canal Zone, where they fought against the British military presence until 1952.

In Cairo, the government had declared martial law on 13 May 1948, on the eve of British withdrawal from Palestine and the proclamation of the State of Israel, and adopted measures against real or alleged allies of the Zionists, exacerbating the pressure on local Jews.[24] Following Israeli air raids on Cairo and Alexandria in June and July 1948, a bomb exploded in the Karaite Jewish quarter, killing some twenty people, and Jewish-owned cinemas, stores and private homes were attacked; in September twenty-nine people were killed in bomb explosions in the Jewish quarter of Cairo; all of these acts of violence were widely attributed to the Muslim Brothers. In October 1948, arms and explosives were found on the country estate (*'izba*) of the head of their Isma'iliyya branch. 15 November 1948 witnessed what became known as the Jeep Affair: a jeep loaded with arms, explosives and confidential papers was intercepted in Cairo and its driver arrested, leading to the disclosure of the Special Apparatus. Hasan al-Banna, who had just returned from the pilgrimage to Mecca, was briefly detained as well. On 4 December 1948, the commander of the Cairo police was shot dead during armed clashes at King Fu'ad (Cairo) University.

In this highly charged atmosphere, al-Banna wondered how the situation should be interpreted – as a *mihna* or a *minha*, a trial or a blessing, for the Muslim community in general and the Muslim Brotherhood in particular.[25] In Mecca, he wrote, believers from all over the world had expressed their admiration for the Muslim Brothers, who did what they themselves did not feel able to accomplish. The strength required was a divine gift (*minha*). If you need encouragement, he told the Brothers, look at the outside world. It is only at home that you are ignored and maligned, for the prophet counts for nothing in his country. In this situation, the example of the Prophet and the early Muslim community should inspire you: you are the "new umma." God willing, the veil shall be lifted and the trial (*mihna*) shall descend upon you. Be steadfast and patient. Fear God and you may yet triumph.

On 8 December 1948, at 11 p.m., the government announced the dissolution of the Society of the Muslim Brothers, who a few months previously had celebrated their twentieth anniversary.[26] The official charge was that a section of the Brotherhood had undergone military training and engaged in terrorist activities; this section was identified with the Rovers – not the Special Apparatus, of which the decree made no mention. The file compiled by the ministry of interior also included charges of instigating social unrest in the countryside, suggesting the Muslim Brothers' link to communism. The Society's headquarters was searched and everyone present was arrested on the spot, except for Hasan al-Banna himself. The

YMMA clubhouse served as a temporary meeting place for the Muslim Brothers. At the time, the Muslim Brotherhood claimed to have up to 500,000 adherents, of whom 40,000 were Rover Scouts; membership in the Special Apparatus was estimated at about 1,000 men. The dissolution order, widespread arrests and the sequestration of their files and property made it all the more difficult for Hasan al-Banna to communicate with members and to control their movements.

On 28 December 1948, Prime Minister al-Nuqrashi was assassinated by a student member of the Ikhwan, who was allegedly inspired by Sayyid Sabiq, a young Azhar shaykh and Muslim Brother. In a fatwa, al-Azhar denounced the murder as a crime against Islam. (The assassin was condemned and hanged in April 1950.) Nuqrashi's successor, Ibrahim 'Abd al-Hadi, took stringent security precautions. Meanwhile al-Banna, fearing for the worst now that the chain of command was broken, tried desperately to reach an understanding with the authorities.[27] At the same time, he protested against the dissolution decree, arguing that the Muslim Brother organization could not be held responsible for the acts of individual members. In a separate memorandum, the Muslim Brothers pointed to the hidden hands of imperialism, world Jewry, the communist International and the agents of immorality and atheism. At the same time they declared that the dissolution decree would have no effect: the Muslim Brothers were "the people," and like a person, they could not be destroyed simply by denying them legal status.

When in January 1949 a Muslim Brother attempted to bomb the courthouse in which the files of the Jeep Affair were held, which included the papers disclosing the workings of the Special Apparatus, al-Banna declared that the men responsible for this crime could not possibly be "either Brothers or Muslims," alienating many of his followers. Further arrests of Muslim Brothers ensued, and there were reports of torture in the prisons. Brutal torture there was, as described by Sharif Hetata (the husband of Egyptian feminist Nawal al-Sa'dawi and not a Muslim Brother) in his novel *The Eye with the Iron Lid*, though many Muslim Brothers were later to say that maltreatment under the monarchy and British rule paled in comparison with what they had to suffer in Nasserist prisons in the 1950s and 1960s.

On 12 February 1949, Hasan al-Banna was shot dead in the street after having been called to the headquarters of the YMMA, most probably by members of the Egyptian secret police.[28] His assassination was followed by a wave of arrests among his family and the Muslim Brothers at large. The authorities prevented anyone except his closest family from attending his burial at the cemetery of Imam al-Shafi'i in Cairo; Makram 'Ubayd, the prominent Coptic politician, was one of the few to defy police orders and pay his condolences to the family. Al-Banna's parents were devastated. Because of his declining eyesight and changing market conditions, Hasan al-Banna's father had given up his business in the early 1940s. After 1949, he resumed the life of a studious recluse, surrounded by books, many of them from India, where the prince of Hyderabad took a special interest in Hadith studies.

4

HASAN AL-BANNA: THE PIVOT OF HIS UNIVERSE

As its founder and General Guide, Hasan al-Banna personified the Society of the Muslim Brothers as no other person did. One of his biographers, and a critical one, noted that "[h]is authority did not derive from social standing, formal learning, rank or age, but was rather a result of his sacrifices and his unrelenting struggle for the Islamic call" (Yusuf, *al-Ikhwan*, 1, p. 7). It is interesting that al-Sayyid Yusuf, the author in question, should not speak of charisma as many others did. Instead he identifies some of the elements that were indeed crucial to al-Banna's rise and success: his energy, dedication and perseverance, combined with his unusual ability to inspire people and motivate them to action. It should be recalled that al-Banna was not a professional politician or community organizer but a schoolteacher who worked full time and directed the Muslim Brothers in his spare time and holidays.

Hasan al-Banna was a man in motion and in transition who lived what he preached: a wholesale commitment to Islam that translated religious conviction into personal conduct and social action. The man did not seem to rest or sleep, and he kept the sort of orderly routine others detested. His world view left no room for subtlety: it was either Islam or perdition, moral integrity or moral dissolution, faith-based power or collective humiliation. Where others spoke of political conflict, party competition or government oppression, al-Banna and the Ikhwan spoke of plots and snares, trials and tribulations, persecution and sedition, *mihna* and *fitna*. Yet in his daily practice as well as his political strategy, al-Banna was cautious and pragmatic, more pragmatic at any rate than his rhetoric suggested. What is perhaps most striking is the element of certainty and continuity that marked his life and career. Every now and then there is a suggestion of despondency or dejection, but not of genuine doubt. There was apparently never a rupture in his life, and no crisis. In his youth he had mentors to show him the way. Thus guided, he recognized his mission at an early age, and his path was clear: the signposts (*ma'alim al-tariq*) Sayyid Qutb had to seek and define appear to have been plainly visible to Hasan al-Banna throughout his life.

Unlike his father, Hasan al-Banna never published a real book. The texts we have constitute functional prose in a variety of formats – speeches, lectures, sermons, "fatwas," open letters and newspaper articles – directed at specific audiences: the Muslim Brothers, attendants at public lectures or political leaders at home and abroad. The journalistic style he employed places al-Banna in the tradition of modern Arab reform movements, which relied heavily on newspapers and periodicals to disseminate their ideas; in al-Banna's time, Arab audiences generally preferred journalistic literature to books (if one excludes the legal and theological classics). In content, however, al-Banna's writings represent the opposite of what most authors of the *nahda*, or Arab revival, aimed at: critical information, reflection and debate. Rather, he aimed for "guidance" and "correct instruction." Hasan al-Banna was a teacher and a preacher: he set forth what was right and true. His father had imbued him with a love of books and learning, and he was well read in the life of the Prophet, Prophetic Traditions, classical Arabic literature and modern reformist thought. Yet in his speeches and writings he referred almost exclusively to the Qur'an and Hadith, mostly taken from the canonical collections. He did not invite theorizing or what he considered superfluous sophistication more generally; in fact, it would not be an exaggeration to describe him as anti-intellectual.

Best known among his writings is the collection of tracts that has been published in numerous editions under the title of *Majmu'at rasa'il al-imam al-shahid Hasan al-Banna* (*The Collected Tracts of the Martyr Imam Hasan al-Banna*). These tracts were either written for specific purposes or based on editorials that originally appeared in the Muslim Brother press. Edited collections of his *Tuesday Talks* (*Hadith al-thalatha'*) were published after his death by members of the Ikhwan. Of special interest is the process of canonization in the course of which al-Banna's oral and written legacy (*turath*) was collected and edited with a critical apparatus. Thus in 2005, the Muslim Brothers' publishing house Dar al-Da'wa issued a series entitled *From the Legacy of Imam al-Banna* (*Min turath al-imam al-Banna*), which included his legal articles and so-called fatwas; also in 2005, *Friday Talks* (*Ahadith al-jum'a*), which originally appeared in the Muslim Brother press, were edited with annotations by 'Isam Talima, the former secretary of Yusuf al-Qaradawi, the noted Muslim scholar–activist. Even more interesting are selected tracts published with comments, on the lines of the classical commentary (*sharh*), especially his tract *Instructions* (*Risalat al-Ta'alim*). Tapes and cassettes of his talks, including those broadcast on Egyptian radio, seem to exist or have existed; however, to the best of my knowledge they have not yet been used for scholarly purposes.

Material on Hasan al-Banna's family background and private life is scarce. His *Memoirs* (*Mudhakkirat al-da'wa wa-l-da'iya*, *Memories of the Mission and the Missionary*) are largely based on articles in the Muslim Brother press and were probably first assembled in 1948 by an unidentified author.[1] If, as it has been argued, they were written in the context of internal conflict over his former friend and associate Ahmad al-Sukkari, this is not clear from the text itself. As the title indicates, the *Memoirs* are not an autobiography. They describe al-Banna's career as an Islamic activist broadly defined, up to his move to Cairo in 1932, followed by scattered notes and documents as well as excerpts from the Muslim Brother press, ending with the outbreak of the Second World War. A diary (*yawmiyyat*) he apparently kept was left unpublished. Information on the al-Banna family derives almost exclusively from Hasan's younger brother Jamal (born 1920), who was able to use their father's diary and other private family materials, including letters and photographs, for his own writings. Among those, the most important are *The Letters of Hasan al-Banna as a Young Man to his Father* (*Khitabat Hasan al-Banna al-shabb ila abihi*), published in 1990.

A rare exception to what I have called Hasan al-Banna's functional prose is a small volume devoted to the *diwan* of Muslim b. al-Walid al-Ansari, called Sari' al-Ghawani ("He who is laid low by the fair maidens"), one of the better-known Arab poets of the early 'Abbasid period, who was born in Kufa around 130–40/747–57 and died in Jurjan, on the Caspian Sea, in 208/823. In addition to his love poetry and the odes and panegyrics on important personalities of his time, Sari' al-Ghawani also wrote satirical verse and drinking songs, two genres one would not have expected al-Banna to have appreciated. Still, al-Banna edited a version of the *diwan* that relied on the Arabic original edited by the Dutch Arabist M. J. de Goeje in 1875. At the end of the little book, which unfortunately is undated, there is a note saying that because of his heavy responsibilities as leader of the Muslim Brotherhood, al-Banna had been unable to check the proofs, and that this task had been accomplished by two competent scholars.

BETWEEN SHAYKH AND *EFENDI*: A SOCIAL PROFILE

Considerable thought has been given to the social and cultural profile of Egypt in the nineteenth and twentieth centuries, from the rule of Muhammad 'Ali (1805–48) and his family, through the British occupation beginning in 1882, to the monarchy (1922–52), and ultimately the era of the Free Officers, Nasser and his successors Anwar al-Sadat and Husni Mubarak, starting in 1952. The categories used have often been of a binary type: urban *v.* rural, traditional *v.* modern, and religious *v.* secular. Like Weberian "ideal types," these categories are not without heuristic value. And yet, like Weberian ideal types, they lose some of their usefulness as soon as one looks at specific persons and social configurations, a fact Weber was perhaps more aware of than some of his later adepts. Most social categories are not fixed and exclusive; they blend into one another, and the blend produces mixed results. Hasan al-Banna serves to illustrate the point, a man of transition in more than one sense.

Hasan al-Banna was characteristic of a large segment of Egyptian society in that his family background was clearly rural, whereas his education, occupation, lifestyle and outlook marked him as an urban person, formed in two towns of quite different character – Damanhur on one hand, and Isma'iliyya on the other – and ultimately in the capital, Cairo. The urban–rural divide was real, but it was also blurred at both ends, with considerable potential for mobility, physical as well as social. The same applies to the distinctions between traditional and modern, and religious and secular, with the latter frequently being identified with an urban existence. The shaykh and the *efendi* are commonly taken as characters representing distinct socio-cultural milieus, one religious and traditional, the other secular and modern. This perception requires refinement.

On both his father's and his mother's side, Hasan al-Banna derived from a rural milieu of comfortable circumstance. Most people would have classified them as fellahin. But fellah (inadequately rendered in English as "peasant") is an elastic term that can refer to a variety of elements, from actual occupation, source of income, residence and lifestyle to ethnic identity and patriotic identification with Egypt.[2] Historians have attempted to identify different classes of landowners and cultivators by looking at their landholdings and have defined as "peasants" all those holding less than ten *feddan*s (one *feddan* equals roughly an acre). There is still some controversy over the dividing line between medium and large landowners, so important in the socio-political life of the country, with some drawing the line at fifty *feddan*s per nuclear family and others at 200 or even 500. However, fifty *feddan*s is the most widely accepted threshold. On his father's side, the al-Banna family belonged to what the Egyptian census listed as "landowners cultivating their own land" (as opposed to "farmers and cultivators"); their landholding is not specified but it must have been less than fifty *feddan*s. Hasan's mother's family was of a similar background; her own father was a merchant in dyed and embroidered fabrics, luxury goods to be sure, but affordable for all but the poorest.

Coming from a fellah family, Hasan al-Banna's father trained as a watchmaker and a religious scholar, representing the well-known type of the artisan-cum-scholar who also engaged in some small-scale trade. Ahmad al-Sa'ati's product – watches, clocks, gramophones and gramophone records – was not really of his own making (unless one counts repairing clocks and watches as such), and it tied him to a modern industry located in the big cities, if not abroad. All his formal education was of the religious kind. This marked him as a shaykh, who combined various official functions with independent study, eventually becoming what in modern academia is called an "independent scholar." As his "family name" he used al-Sa'ati, referring to his profession. It was only after he had given up his craft that he reverted to al-Banna. The sons went a different way: Hasan trained with his father as a clockmaker but was always known as al-Banna, whereas his younger brother 'Abd al-Rahman, who held a degree in commerce and worked for a steam engine company, mostly went by the name al-Sa'ati.

It appears that in contrast to national leaders like Sa'd Zaghlul, a lawyer of rural background who had married into high society, who proudly called himself "a peasant son of a peasant" (*fallah ibn fallah*), Hasan al-Banna never called himself a fellah. Nonetheless, his career bears out the close ties between town and countryside so typical of the period, with its easy transition from village notable or rural middle class to urban *efendi*. In terms of his education, al-Banna was a product of the middle path or "cross-over," combining *kuttab* and government schooling in a field – that is, the Arabic language – that retained core elements of traditional learning, from the subject matter that was closely tied to Qur'anic recitation, to the methods of instruction that continued to be premised on rote learning. In certain ways, al-Banna moved between the shaykh and the *efendi*, and this ambiguity was reflected in the titles he assumed and the clothing he chose to wear, an issue that comes up repeatedly in his career. Dress could be especially expressive of social identity, including notably the headgear (turban or fez, *tarbush*), footwear (sandals, slippers or shoes), and outer clothing (*jallabiyya* and cloak, *aba'a*, or European suit). Al-Banna's father was a shaykh and dressed like one, even in Cairo, with a *jallabiyya*, an *aba'a* and the distinctive turban of the Egyptian religious scholar, even though according to photographs from the 1940s he wore shoes rather than sandals.

Hasan himself made an interesting transition from ordinary village attire, to consciously chosen *salafi* garb, to modern *efendi* clothes with Islamic references, and he was very conscious of that fact, commenting on it in his *Letters* and *Memoirs*.[3] The first anecdote concerns his time at the elementary teachers' training school in Damanhur in the early 1920s. In his *Memoirs* he recalls how one day the inspector came to the school and surveyed his appearance with visible displeasure: it combined a turban, sandals of the type worn by pilgrims during the *hajj* and a white cloak over the *jallabiyya*. Questioned as to what this was about, Hasan declared that it was the practice (*sunna*) of the Prophet. In other words, it was the *salafi* way. The inspector then enquired, rather maliciously, whether he followed all other Prophetic practices as well. No, said Hasan, this was not possible yet but he was doing his best. To this the inspector rejoined that the governorate would not allow him to teach in this outfit because it would alienate the pupils.

The second anecdote concerns Dar al-'Ulum, where Western dress was adopted in the mid-1920s. According to al-Banna, the decision caused much agitation among students and faculty. In the end only two students persisted in wearing the *jallabiyya* and turban rather than the suit and *tarbush*, and he was one of them. The director told them that it would not be good if the class were to appear divided, some wearing the turban and the others the *tarbush*. Out of respect for him rather than out of conviction Hasan and his colleague finally donned the suit and *tarbush*: Hasan al-Banna would not have yielded to the rules imposed by an institution, but he could do so out of respect for a teacher.

By the time he arrived in Isma'iliyya to teach Arabic at a primary school, al-Banna's taste had evolved. By ordinary standards, he was an *efendi*, a member of the "modern," educated middle class, and he dressed as an *efendi*, with a European suit and a silken pocket handkerchief, a *tarbush*, and a bottle of eau de cologne next to his bed. He adopted his characteristic austere style only later when touring the Egyptian countryside for the Muslim Brothers, when he reverted to the *jallabiyya*, white cloak and turban. The suit and *tarbush* were, of course, the required attire of the government employee, and as a schoolteacher al-Banna represented the modern state. What distinguished him from the ordinary *efendi* was his well-groomed beard, which expressed his conscious attempt to create some kind of Islamic appearance – "Islamic modern," so to speak. There is no indication that adopting the basic elements of modern living with respect to clothing, furniture and eating habits created any problem for him.

Matters were different for his parents, who like many rural migrants found life in the capital difficult, even in the more popular neighbourhoods of Cairo. For years, the family seems to have lived under some strain, which was not solely of a financial nature. Many times they changed their residence, although they always remained in the area between al-Khalifa, Sayyida Zaynab and al-Darb al-Ahmar, and these moves cannot have been easy, involving as they did several children. While the family may not have possessed many pieces of furniture and other household items, there were Shaykh Ahmad's books and manuscripts, which required some special attention. There can be little doubt that their neighbours saw them as fellahin: they used a *tabaliyya*, a large tray that was put on the floor, not a table, and they usually ate with their hands and a spoon, not a fork and knife. Rural people considered this the Islamic way of doing things. In al-Mahmudiyya, life had been less regulated, and the children had grown up "like plants in the field" (*Letters*, p. 46); in Cairo, life was more constrained.

Shaykh Ahmad devoted most of his time to his studies and the proceeds from his shop cannot have amounted to much. The additional income he derived from renting his house and shop in al-Mahmudiyya was threatened when, during the Great Depression of

1929–32, the tenants could no longer pay their rent. Nevertheless, the parents always remained able to keep a servant or household help, but it was only from 1941 onwards that the father refers to payments of the *zakat* in his diary, suggesting a certain ease; nonetheless their lifestyle remained frugal if not austere. The widening gap in lifestyle and habits between parents and eldest son becomes clear when one reads Hasan's letters to his father, in which he asked or indeed instructed the latter to take good care of the children and to make sure they prayed correctly, kept clean and did not walk barefoot; he also recommended that the family keep to a regular schedule for meals and distinguish between the functions of different rooms (*Letters*, pp. 112f.).

Hasan al-Banna was not modest when it came to his self-appointed role as preacher and guide, rousing his people from slumber and pointing the way to salvation. But he lived modestly. His simplicity of style and manners impressed many and endeared him to his followers (Anwar al-Jundi quoted from Lia, *Society*, p. 119):

> What distinguishes this man most of all is the fact that he has kept a particular bearing throughout his life. This quality surpasses his dignity, greatness, manliness, honour, spiritual purity and noble character. This particular bearing is his simple austere lifestyle, devoid of all kinds of luxury, snobbery, haughtiness, wealth and personal glory.

But to what extent did Hasan al-Banna's social background and the social base of the Muslim Brothers influence or even determine the moral and ideological choices the group espoused?

ISLAM APPLIED: AN INTELLECTUAL PROFILE

Hasan al-Banna was not an original thinker if he can be called a thinker at all. Given his pointedly anti-intellectual stance, one hesitates to do so. He was an activist who essentially "put to work" what

Muslim reformers had advocated for decades, though he did so in his own way. Like other social and political actors, Islamists learn from experience, they interact with others to articulate their ideas, drawing on earlier as well as contemporary intellectual trends, and they design their strategies accordingly. For this reason, al-Banna's discourse cannot be read in isolation; it requires the tools of "relational history" to be properly assessed. This calls for close attention to the historical context, not least to avoid an Islamic exceptionalism of the kind propagated by the Islamists themselves. As mentioned above, three elements acted as formative influences on Hasan al-Banna as a young man: (Arab) reform Islam of the Salafi type, popular Sufism of the "sober" kind and Egyptian patriotism. Inevitably, he was also in touch with contemporary thought more generally, and this included first and foremost Western thought. The special blend that resulted from the interplay of these elements is particularly evident in his notions of self-help and communal identity. A detailed analysis would require careful attendance to the gradual evolution of his ideas, style and terminology, and the precise context in which they evolved. Here, "close reading" and "thick description" will have to be sacrificed to the demands of a broad survey.

In view of his self-perception as a man with a clearly defined mission, it is ironic that al-Banna should have been so consistently accused of "obscurity" (*ghumud*); he himself was fully aware of this accusation.[4] This "obscurity," however, did not detract from his appeal to educated or semi-educated urban youth, or to be even more precise, to semi-educated young urban males. On the contrary, a certain degree of imprecision made it easier to attract attention and maintain internal unity. Generally speaking, it is as useful to look at what al-Banna was *against* – vice or "the forbidden" writ large, licentiousness, permissiveness, foreign domination, Christian mission, materialism, secularism and communism – as what he stood *for*.

According to W. Cantwell Smith, the Muslim Brothers represented "a determination … to get back to a basis for society of accepted moral standards and integrated vision, and to go forward to a programme of active implementation of popular goals by an effectively organized corps of disciplined and devoted idealists." Through this they sought to "transform Islam … into an operative force actively at work on modern problems" (*Islam in Modern History*, pp. 156f.). As Brynjar Lia put it, they propagated a "new understanding of Islam as an all-encompassing concept on which a comprehensive ideology could be based, including a search for renewal and novel interpretations which would make Islam relevant to modern Muslims" (*Society*, p. 86). Gregory Starrett spoke of a "functionalization of religion – putting it consciously to work for various types of social and political projects" (*Putting Islam to Work*, p. 10). In other words, the Muslim Brothers and Hasan al-Banna more particularly used Islam as a resource to produce (create, mould) a new personality and community based on faith. Did this "functionalization" constitute a new or novel understanding of Islam? If compared to thinkers of the classical and post-classical ages, certainly, but not if placed in a contemporary context.

What al-Banna fought for and against had been at the heart of Islamic reformism since the 1870s, constituting the Salafi classics, so to speak. Religion in general and Islam in particular were not merely one of several domains of life, or one "field" among others, to use Pierre Bourdieu's terminology: it provided the moral foundation of community and society. The Salafis called on Muslims to wake up, to shake off the dead weight of the past and to face the challenges of modernity, the age in which they were living, while holding fast to true Islam. They denounced Muslim weakness, factionalism, imitation and moral dissolution, and advocated Muslim self-confidence, unity, strength, pride and action. So did Hasan al-Banna. The Muslim Brothers propagated an activist stance, appealing to the individual to act jointly with others to combat social inertia and political quietism; they called for Islamic unity in all its dimensions – political, legal and theological – and they worked for the liberation of Egypt, the "Eastern nations" and the Islamic community.

In this framework, Islam served as a source of entitlement and empowerment, of the oppressed vis-à-vis the oppressor and the colonized vis-à-vis the colonizer. Islam, the Muslim community and the Egyptian nation were weak and despised because of internal division combined with the onslaught of imperialism and un-Islamic ideas introduced from outside. But Islam had the potential to liberate Egypt and the Muslim community and indeed to save humanity. This required a programme of individual and communal reform, struggle and total dedication, involving *da'wa* as well as *jihad*. If Muslims were ready to face this task and take up the burden, they could triumph.

Hasan al-Banna shared the ambivalence towards the West and modernity – if ambivalence is the right word – of most Islamic thinkers of the late nineteenth and early twentieth centuries. He, too, offered the characteristic blend of Islamic and modern (Western) references, whether openly acknowledged or not; he, too, did not hesitate to quote Western authors when it suited his purposes. Rather than saying that he adopted an ambivalent stance, it would perhaps be more appropriate to say that he judged with discrimination, distinguishing between the West at home (where it championed modern science and parliamentary democracy) and the West abroad (where it acted as a colonial power). If religion is the moral foundation of society, then what can be good for one society may be bad for another, irrespective of whether the relevant elements – political parties or specific forms of cultural expression – have been freely adopted or forcibly imposed. What is required is a selective and pragmatic approach, based on a utilitarian logic that adopts what is useful and rejects what is not. The Ikhwan's propagation of modern science and technology is entirely consistent with this approach. But what are the standards of usefulness? Hasan al-Banna does not probe into the question.

For him, the important thing was the right frame of mind with which to face the West. He deeply resented the conspicuous contempt with which many Europeans treated Muslims and Egyptians alike, and he was aggrieved by what he saw as Muslim servility. Muslims, he believed, must free themselves of their submissiveness and inferiority complex vis-à-vis the West and stop imitating

Western models.[5] He was afraid that outsiders who knew little about Islam and looked at the conditions of its people were led to believe that Islam was a religion of lowliness and apathy, weakness and resignation. In a similar vein, he drew a parallel to the People of Israel under the rule of Pharaoh, an overbearing despot who enslaved God's worshippers, despising them, a noble and glorious people, and using them as his slaves and servants. In his *Memoirs* he recounted the surprise and indeed repentance of supercilious Europeans who were put to shame by upright Egyptian citizens: a plumber who refused to accept a bribe, *baqshish*, a carpenter who charged a fair price and nothing but ... "Eject imperialism from your souls," he said more than once, "and it will leave your land."

It is in this context that one has to place the fury directed at Christian missionaries from America and Europe, who had been one of the chief concerns of Muslim reformers and a concern shared by the Eastern Christian churches, as they were the principal target of Western missionary efforts. Christian mission in Egypt remains to be studied more comprehensively, and it is still difficult to obtain empirical data on its scope and impact. It appears that conversion was not very significant among Orthodox Copts and very rare among Muslims. Even so, missionary influence in the fields of education, health, philanthropy and associational life in Egypt as well as elsewhere in the Middle East was profound, acting as an important stimulus to similar activities among Muslim "reformers."[6] The focus of the Muslim Brothers on Islamic education, charitable work and moral uplift as well as their choice of style and method, from coffeehouse preaching to village tours to homiletic tracts, testifies to the deep impact of missionary practices on modern *da'wa*. Equally worthy of note is the framing of Muslim reaction to the missionary challenge, which portrayed missionary activity as a Christian plot to weaken Muslim society and Islam at large by "corrupting" its weakest members: women and children. By the same token, it rendered these Muslim nations impotent in the face of Western imperialism, for Muslim faith and national integrity were intimately connected. Not only in Egypt were women and the nation portrayed as vulnerable victims of foreign encroachment. The representation of the nation *as a woman* constituted a topos of nationalist discourse in many countries; France is a prime example. It should be added that the fear was not entirely unfounded, for, like modern developmentalists, missionaries (many of whom were themselves women) often did target women to make an impact on society at large.

Sufism deserves a final remark. The importance of Sufism for Hasan al-Banna's personal development is undisputed. The question is to what extent Sufism shaped his socio-political thought and activities, and, moving beyond him as an individual, to what extent it mattered to the way the Muslim Brothers functioned. Al-Banna never denied his youthful fascination with Sufi *dhikr* and visits to the tombs of holy men, and throughout his life he retained his respect for the Sufi masters who had inspired him in his youth. But as an adult he felt that, like Islam as a whole, Sufism was in need of a process of cleansing and renewal on the lines advocated by the Salafi reformers.[7] The Muslim Brotherhood initially operated as an Islamic benevolent society with a strong Sufi element. At some point, al-Banna even declared that the Hasafi Benevolent Society in al-Mahmudiyya had served as the nucleus of the Muslim Brotherhood. Certain practices of the Ikhwan and their basic terminology were clearly informed by Sufi teachings; prayers of the kind contained in al-Banna's *Risalat al-Ma'thurat*, for instance, formed a characteristic element of Sufi devotions. In Isma'iliyya, the Sufi element was still distinctive, and even after the move to Cairo, weekly lectures on ethics and Sufism were held at the headquarters, and branches were instructed to hold a Judgement Day (*yawm al-akhira*) once a month when the Brothers were to visit the tombs of saints. In his *Risalat al-Ta'alim*, al-Banna explicitly allowed such visits but condemned hopes for the intercession of the dead, *tawassul*. *Dhikr* and night vigils were part of the training of the Rovers and the Battalions. Even so, Sufi practices were criticized by educated urban Muslim Brothers. Salafi critics spoke deprecatingly of "dervishism." By the 1940s the condemnation of Sufism had become commonplace among Muslim Brothers, highlighting the thorough transformation of the movement.

WHAT WENT WRONG?

Hasan al-Banna's view of Islamic history as a continuous decline from the glorious times of the Prophet, his Companions and the Rightly Guided Caliphs, a decline linked to the debilitating influences of non-Arabs on Muslim society and civilization, was conventional and conflicted with his egalitarian beliefs that forbade placing Arab Muslims above non-Arab Muslims. Equally conventional was his idealization of the early Muslim conquests. But this conventional view was at odds with the idea of progress since the age of the Prophet, which he also advocated, when he presented history as analogous to human development, moving from ignorant childhood to youth, maturity and knowledge. A lengthy quote from *Our Mission* (*Da'watuna*) can perhaps convey an idea of his train of thought and the passion of his style:[8]

> Experience and events have taught us that the disease afflicting these Eastern nations has various aspects and numerous symptoms that have done harm to every expression of their lives. Politically, they have been assailed by imperialism on the part of their enemies, and by factionalism, enmity, division and disunity among their own members. Economically, they have been assailed by the spread of usurious practices among all social classes, and the usurpation of their natural resources and wealth by foreign companies. Intellectually, they have been afflicted by anarchy, defection and heresy which destroy their religious beliefs and shatter the supreme ideal in the souls of their sons. Socially, they have been assailed by licentiousness of manners and mores, and the dissolution of the bond of humane virtues they inherited from their glorious ancestors. Through imitation of the West, the viper's venom creeps into their lives, poisoning their blood and sullying the purity of their happiness. They have been assailed through positive law which does not deter the criminal, chastise the aggressor or repel the unjust ... They have been assailed through anarchy in their educational policies, which makes it impossible to guide their children correctly, their men of the future and those who will be responsible for bringing about their renaissance. Psychologically, they have been afflicted with deadly

> despair, murderous apathy, shameful cowardice, ignoble humility and all-pervading effemination, meanness and egotism which prevent people from making any effort, preclude sacrifice and thrust the nation from the ranks of fighters to those of trifling players.
>
> What hope is there for a nation against which all these elements, in their strongest manifestations and most extreme forms, have united for the assault – imperialism and factionalism, usury and foreign companies, heresy, licentiousness and anarchy in education and legislation, despair and meanness, impotence and cowardice, combined with admiration for the enemy, an admiration that invites wholesale imitation, especially of his evil deeds?

The immediate past was thus marred by a lack of faith exacerbated by the onslaught of imperialism and the infiltration of alien ideas. But al-Banna held an optimistic view of human potential: if community and nation unite, the tide can be turned, wrong can be righted and order restored. Islam will not be destroyed even under the most adverse circumstances:[9]

> The tenets and teachings of Islam remained powerful in themselves, abundantly fertile and vital, attractive and enchanting in their splendour and beauty. They will remain so because they are the truth, and human existence will never achieve perfection and virtue through any other means because they are of God's creation.

Islam is the consummation of prophecy for which humankind (al-Banna would actually have said "mankind") has been slowly prepared and perfected; the Muslim community is "the best nation that has been brought forth to humankind" (Q3:110). Hasan al-Banna harboured a grandiose vision of Muslims as the saviours of humankind, corresponding to Western imperialist notions of the white man's burden: Muslims were morally bound to save the nation, the "East" and humanity at large. This was the burden they had to shoulder. The Qur'an, he wrote in his tract *To What Do We Summon People?*:[10]

> placed a higher duty on their shoulders: to guide humankind to truth, to lead all people to the good, and to illuminate the whole world with

> the sun of Islam ... This means that the Noble Qur'an appoints the Muslims as guardians over humankind which is still in its minority, and grants them the right of sovereignty and dominion over the world in order to carry out this noble mandate. Hence, it is our concern not that of the West and it belongs to the civilization of Islam not the civilization of materialism.

THE MEANS OF CHANGE

If Islam was the key to salvation and human happiness, what was the role of the Muslim Brothers in this larger scheme? From an early date, Hasan al-Banna displayed a pronounced sense of mission, and the Muslim Brothers followed his example: we are the people, we stand for Islam. Al-Banna conceived of the Muslim Brothers as a spiritual elite, a vanguard whose mission it was to rouse the dormant Muslim masses and the Egyptian people in particular. In a remarkable adaptation of colonial representations of the colonized as fatalistic, lazy and passive, leading reformists spoke of the stupor Muslims had fallen victim to; the term *ghafla* signifies slumber as well as carelessness and indifference. This *ghafla* implied more than a lack of awareness; it revealed a spiritual torpor, that is to say, a moral failing, and it called for a broad programme of moral reconstruction. Rashid Rida said so in the pages of *al-Manar*. In his tract *Our Mission* (*Da'watuna*), al-Banna proclaimed:[11]

> The difference between us and our people (*qawm*), though we agree on our faith in this principle [Islam], is that among them it is an anaesthetized faith, dormant within their souls, one to whose law they do not wish to submit and according to whose rule they do not wish to act; whereas it is a burning, blazing, intense faith fully awakened in the souls of the Muslim Brothers.

As was mentioned above, Hasan al-Banna advocated a gradualist approach that would allow people to mend their ways until they had fully embraced the tenets of Islam as understood by the Muslim Brothers. He told his fellow Ikhwan to correct errors with gentleness, and not to act like the zealots found in other Islamic associations. One of the recurrent metaphors in this context is that of illness and treatment, *al-da' wa-l-dawa'*. Thus al-Banna wrote in one of his *Friday Talks*: "In your hands, and yours alone, o ye heirs of the prophets and the messengers and those who brought forth the signs of the Lord of Lords, is the bottle of medicine. Are you going to be the doctor and treat yourselves and bring the medicine to the others?"[12]

Yet al-Banna also propagated *jihad*.[13] In fact, reference to struggle, fight, sacrifice, combat and *jihad* – including, if necessary, armed struggle against the enemies of Islam – pervades his entire discourse. Richard Mitchell has highlighted the importance of militancy and martyrdom, expressed not only in a military idiom, but in the distinctive "tone" permeating everything – al-Banna's speeches and writings as well as the activities of the Rovers and Battalions, not to mention the Special Apparatus. While it is true that most relevant texts date from the late 1930s and the 1940s, it is not possible to establish a clear chronological sequence, with later statements abrogating, as it were, earlier ones, for al-Banna frequently made conflicting statements at more or less the same time, though not necessarily on the same occasion. Between December 1936 and January 1937, he wrote a number of editorials on *The Military Spirit in Islam* (*al-Jundiyya fi l-islam*). A decade later, in 1947, he sent an open letter to King Faruq and other Arab and Muslim leaders, entitled *To the Light* (*Nahwa l-nur*). Here he argued:[14]

> the renascent nations need power (*quwwa*), and need to implant the military spirit (or militarism, *jundiyya*) in their sons ... Islam did not overlook this factor, but made it a mandatory obligation, and did not differentiate in any way between it (this military spirit) and prayer and fasting. In the entire world, there is no system, past or present, that has concerned itself with this factor to the extent that Islam has in the Qur'an ... The modern nations have paid close attention to this military spirit, and have based themselves on these principles. Thus we see that Mussolini's Fascism, Hitler's Nazism and Stalin's Communism are based on pure militarism. But there is a vast difference between

> all of these and the military spirit of Islam, for Islam, which has so thoroughly sanctified power, has given preference to peace.

Note that in the present context, al-Banna uses the neologism *jundiyya*, not *jihad*. This is not to say that he avoided the term. On the contrary, he published widely on *jihad*, covering the broad range of meanings from self-discipline to armed struggle, also described in the Islamic tradition as the "greater" and the "lesser" *jihad*. *Jihad* was and still is a keyword denoting all kinds of endeavours aimed at bettering the condition of the Muslim individual and the Muslim community, and it could easily be transferred from the defence of the Muslim community to anti-colonial struggle and national liberation. Thus 13 November 1918, the day an Egyptian delegation met the British high commissioner and formed al-Wafd al-Misri to represent the nation in London, was known as Jihad Day, Yawm al-Jihad. Hasan al-Banna wrote on many occasions on spiritual or psychological *jihad*, *al-jihad al-nafsani* as he called it. Yet it is beyond doubt that in many instances he spoke of armed struggle, not self-discipline and the "purification of souls." His *Risalat al-Ta'alim* and his speech at the Fifth General Conference in 1939 are cases in point. His tract *On Jihad*, written in the latter part of the 1930s and required reading for the Muslim Brothers, could not have been more explicit. After lengthy quotations from the Qur'an, Sunna and scholarly literature, al-Banna concluded by saying (*Rasa'il*, p. 260):

> You can see from all this how the scholars, both those who employed independent judgement and those who followed precedent (*al-mujtahidun wa-l-muqallidun*), the earliest and their successors, agree unanimously that *jihad* is a collective duty imposed upon the Muslim community in order to spread the call (to Islam), and an individual duty to repulse the attacks of unbelievers upon it. As you know, the Muslims are today forced to humble themselves before non-Muslims, and are ruled by infidels. Their lands have been trampled over, and their honour has been violated. Their enemies govern their affairs, and the rites of their religion have fallen into abeyance within their own lands, to say nothing of their impotence to spread the call. Hence it

> has become an imperative individual duty for every Muslim to prepare himself for *jihad* until the opportunity arises and God decrees a matter that shall be accomplished ... I should mention to you that before the present age of darkness in which their pride has died, the Muslims never abandoned *jihad* throughout history, nor did they neglect it, not even their religious scholars, Sufis, artisans and others. All were fully prepared.

A decade later, he was even more specific. In an article for *Jaridat al-Ikhwan al-Muslimin*, he wrote in October 1946 (*Ahadith al-jum'a*, p. 77):

> If today Islam and its lands are in the state that the Muslims perceive perfectly well: a divided plunder in the hands of the plunderers and the object of desire of the covetous, then *jihad* is now a stringent duty (*farida muhkama*) and a binding necessity. Their rulers and leaders must lead them and summon them to war, and they shall earn glory and support in this world, and shall be rewarded with paradise in the other.

This could be read as an endorsement of national liberation, with armed struggle directed against the foreign enemy, be it the British or the Zionists in neighbouring Palestine. Did al-Banna also advocate the use of force against domestic enemies, Muslims as well as non-Muslims? The answer is less clear. True, he recommended gradualism and national unity; but what he said in his tract *On Jihad* leaves ample room for interpretation:[15]

> God ordained *jihad* for the Muslims not as a tool of oppression or a means of satisfying personal ambitions, but rather as a defence of the call (to spread Islam), a guarantee of peace, and a means for implementing the great message, the burden of which the Muslims bear, the message guiding humankind to truth and justice. For Islam, even as it ordains war, extols peace.

His celebration of "the art of death," *fann al-mawt*, and of "death as art," *al-mawt fann*, has gained special notoriety.[16] It first occurred in an article written for *al-Nadhir* in 1357/1937, during the Arab Revolt in Palestine, when al-Banna used the term "the craft of death," *sina'at al-mawt*; he did the same in his tract *On Jihad*. In a reprint for *Jaridat al-Ikhwan al-Muslimin*, in Ramadan 1365/1946, he replaced this term with the better-known *fann al-mawt*. His glorification of the early Muslim conquests confirms the unconditional admiration for the military spirit of the earliest generations of Muslims, *al-salaf al-salih*. Major battles – first and foremost Badr – were commemorated by the Ikhwan, including poetry and theatrical productions, because commemoration "benefited the Muslims." Again it should be remembered that in the mid-1930s, writing on the early Muslim era was very much in vogue; Muhammad Husayn Haykal is perhaps the best-known example of the liberal man of letters turning to Islamic themes. On occasion al-Banna called for the Islamic empire of the early period to be restored. There was apparently nothing wrong with empires based on conquest, provided they were of the right kind, and, for him, the early Muslim conquests decidedly were. In *To What Do We Summon People?*, he asserted:[17]

> The Muslim conqueror was a teacher endowed with the light, guidance, mercy and compassion with which the teacher must be graced, and the Islamic conquest was a conquest that brought civilization, culture, guidance and education. How can this be compared with what Western imperialism is doing at the present time?

In his tract *Our Mission*, he even speaks of "sacred conquests" (*futuh muqaddasa*). But in contrast to later Islamists such as Sayyid Qutb, al-Banna did not invite *takfir*, excluding believers from the Muslim community and declaring *jihad* against them licit. In his *Risalat al-Ta'alim*, he explicitly rejected *takfir* (*Rasa'il*, p. 271). For him, being "dormant" was not the same as being an infidel. Al-Banna always retained his faith in the piety of Egyptian men and women. In a telling anecdote in his *Memoirs*, he wrote about a young and barely educated peasant who knew a lot about Ahmad al-Badawi, the Muslim saint buried in Tanta. How many hidden treasures similar to this simple peasant, he wondered, were there to be found and put to use in Egypt (*Memoirs*, pp. 38–40)? Even so, al-Banna's militant rhetoric was frequently at odds with his cautious policies, and his ultimate intentions were difficult to discern, for his followers as much as for outside observers, scholars included.

ON UNITY AND COMMUNITY

What is the "imagined community" Hasan al-Banna was thinking of and working for? The question is not always easy to answer, for in his writings Islamic belonging, Arab identity and Egyptian patriotism are difficult to disentangle, the more so since in his later years al-Banna seemed to think of overlapping circles, stretching from Egypt, the Arab nation and the (vaguely defined) East or Orient to the Muslim community and ultimately humanity at large. The centrality of unity to his world view is uncontested: faith, he declared, is unity; fragmentation and disunity equal unbelief, for the Prophet said, "the believers are like one body." The established legal schools (*madhahib*) quibble over trivialities, and theological issues act as minefields. Muslims must bridge the Sufi–Salafi divide as well as the Sunni–Shi'i rift. On many occasions, al-Banna invoked the ideal of a community beyond race and class, building on the tradition of what has been called "Islamic egalitarianism" (Marlow). Accordingly, all men have one common origin, and the Arab has no precedence over the non-Arab. In the 1930s, al-Banna openly repudiated fascist and Nazi racism.[18] With modern means of communication, he wrote, when people can have breakfast in New York, lunch in London and dinner in India, the world is ready for unity. Islam can provide the foundation for this unity.

Al-Banna's conceptualization of community, nation, homeland and citizenship (*umma*, *watan*, *jinsiyya*) poses a challenge, for his use of the terms remained vague and confusing. Like certain Salafi authors before him, al-Banna did not hesitate to speak of an Islamic "nationality" or "citizenship" (*jinsiyya*) creating a bond among all residents of the Islamic homeland. This rested on a transposition of territorial concepts of Islamic belonging, from the "abode of Islam" (*dar al-Islam*) of classical Islamic law and theology to modern (nationalist) concepts of the homeland or fatherland. In 1934, al-Banna wrote in *Jaridat al-Ikhwan al-Muslimin*:[19]

> Every piece of land where the banner of Islam has been hoisted is the fatherland of the Muslims ... It is a duty incumbent on every Muslim to struggle towards the aim of making all people Muslim and the whole world Islamic, so that the banner of Islam can flutter over the earth and the call of the muezzin can resound in all the corners of the world: God is greatest!

This idea was subsequently developed in *Our Mission* (*Da'watuna*), where al-Banna presented a vision of several mutually reinforcing circles, or steps: the liberation of Egypt and the instalment of an Islamic order there was to be followed by the struggle for Arab unity as the basis of Islamic unity and ultimately the establishment of Islamic hegemony and the brotherhood of humankind. In spite of its relevance to Egyptian politics in the 1920s and 1930s, or perhaps precisely because of it, the caliphate plays no prominent role in his vision of the future, even though on occasion he described the restoration of the caliphate as the final goal of Islamic struggle.

If the relation between Islam and Arabism or the Arab nation remained unclear, constituting a prime example of the "obscurity" al-Banna was accused of, there is no doubt that the Egyptian nation occupied the central place in his political imaginary. As earlier Salafi authors had said, "patriotism is part of faith" (*hubb al-watan min al-iman*); al-Banna declared again and again that patriotism was "ordained by God" and that Egypt played a unique role in Islam.[20] It is helpful to compare his notion of universalism to nationalist claims to represent the one and undivided nation. Both are framed in terms of territorially defined socio-cultural units. Hasan al-Banna did not invent the exalted tone of nationalism, with its invocation of sacred duty and sacred home, sacred bond and sacred trust, so dear to nationalists of all kinds, including the "secular" Wafd. Sa'd Zaghlul equally spoke of a "sacred duty" he had to fulfil. In light of Islamist deprecations of the pre-Islamic period as the "age of ignorance," *jahiliyya*, al-Banna's positive comments about pharaonic Egypt merit attention. But what is the place of non-Muslims in the Islamic homeland, and in Egypt more specifically? Al-Banna was not clear on the subject, or perhaps not consistent. His reassurances to Egyptian Copts that they were the brothers and fellow countrymen of Muslims are one thing; his statements on religious freedom, apostasy and national loyalty another. If, as he asserted, religion – that is, Islam – was at the core of Egyptian society, to abandon one's religion was to forsake one's identity, betraying both nation and community. The conflict between these statements remained unresolved.

ISLAM AS A SYSTEM

Hasan al-Banna pursued an integrated approach that went from the individual to the family to society to humankind, the details of which, however, were only gradually worked out. Predictably enough, attention has largely focused on his ideas of good governance and his position on violence in general and *jihad* in particular. The two undoubtedly deserve to be studied, though there are other dimensions to his thought, notably his concept of New Islamic Man and Woman, which have perhaps been unduly neglected. At the core of his project lies the conviction that Islam is a system, *nizam*. A closer look reveals that he does not use the term consistently; in some instances, *nizam* stands for the unchanging divine order and in others for the Islamic order to be established in accordance with the changing requirements of time and place. This Islamic order cannot be reduced to an Islamic state or government, even though the state is crucial to its functioning. It is precisely in this close link to the modern nation state that the specifically modern character of al-Banna's socio-political project comes out most clearly.

For al-Banna, Islam is universal, eternal and all-encompassing (*'alami*, *khalid*, *shumuli*); it is simple and straightforward; easy, not intended to make things hard for humans; and practical, comprising not just faith, dogma and ritual obligations, but work and action (*'amal*). In his tract *Our Mission*, he declared (*Rasa'il*, p. 16):

> Our mission is one described most comprehensively by the term "Islamic." This word has a broad meaning, unlike the meaning normally understood by people. We believe that Islam is an all-embracing concept which regulates all aspects of life, providing for every one of its concerns and prescribing for it a fixed and detailed order.

This conviction was expressed in different words over and over again. Thus al-Banna wrote in November 1946 (*Ahadith al-jum'a*, p. 98):

> It is characteristic of this message that it laid down the affairs of this world and the hereafter, that it is religion and state, spirit and matter, work and culture, divine law and statute, a complete and precise system that is beneficial to the individual, the home [family], community, state and the world ... The Qur'an put general principles (*al-kulliyyat*) before you, and traced the signposts for you (*ma'alim al-tariq*). Whoever travels on the road will reach his destination, and who is led by the light of God will not go astray.

In an article on revolution, published in September 1946, he argued against those who thought that Islam was merely about spirituality and religious obligations, or *din* narrowly defined. But no: Islam was truly comprehensive, *kamil shamil*, and constituted a greater revolution in human life and history than the French or the Russian revolutions (*Ahadith al-jum'a*, pp. 72–5).

A MORAL ORDER, OR CREATING NEW ISLAMIC MAN

As Brynjar Lia has argued, linking religious and moral issues to national concerns was the decisive element that distinguished the Muslim Brothers from all other social and political forces in Egypt (*Society*, p. 213). Morality has to be seen as a comprehensive concept that is most easily defined through its opposites, corruption or moral dissolution. Hasan al-Banna did not underrate the importance of material resources in achieving the desired liberation from foreign domination. But he put even greater emphasis on interior strength or moral fibre, and was convinced of the ability of men to improve their lot through their own efforts. Expressed in more fashionable terms, he believed in agency and the necessary training of human resources. Hasan al-Banna thoroughly embraced the nineteenth-century faith in self-help and moral improvement. But he did not adopt the liberal credo of rugged individualism. His aim was not to promote the unfettered development of the individual and his or her personality, but to *form* the self and *reform* the community in order to render them useful and effective – for the ideal Islamic order to be established in the here and now.

There was nothing original in the idea of moral betterment, or uplift, a cornerstone of reformist thought in the Muslim world as much as in Europe and the West at large. To design the required efforts at cultivating and purifying the self and others, al-Banna employed a cluster of terms (*tarbiya*, *tadhib*, *tanshi'*), all pointing to the need for self-cultivation through discipline. He frequently cited the Qur'an, which in Sura 13:11 says "Verily never will God change the condition of a people until they change it themselves." This put a heavy responsibility on their shoulders, and al-Banna frequently referred to this "burden" to be shouldered by the vanguard of devoted Muslims, and declared his readiness to do so even at great personal expense. The Qur'anic principle to "enjoin good and prohibit wrong" (*al-amr bil-ma'ruf wa-l-nahy 'ani l-munkar*) had inspired him from an early age.

It is tempting to identify traces of Sufi teachings, rooting the call for self-help and improvement in this important strand of the Islamic tradition. But the differences must not be glossed over, either: it is not introspection and self-purification that al-Banna is concerned with, but an active involvement in the world, with energies directed outward, not inward. Note the telling anecdote of his encounter with a young Sufi shaykh, when he was still a young teacher in Isma'iliyya: what do you do, he asked the shaykh, when the Sufi meeting is over? Is there anything that remains? What matters is the following: "knowledge, order and discipline, education in the light of our pious ancestors and the history of our hero-warriors" (*Memoirs*, p. 72).

At the same time, one cannot overlook the impact of nineteenth-century ideas of moral betterment as developed in Europe and America, and exported through various channels to the Middle East. Christians were exposed to it as were Jews; the influence of Jewish Enlightenment (Haskala) and modern concepts of moral reform on Jewish communities in the Ottoman Empire offer interesting parallels. Muslims did not remain unaffected by these ideas, either, and it is not without irony that it was Western missionaries, whose nefarious influence the Muslim Brothers fought so tenaciously, that acted as their main vehicle of transmission.

The famous book by the Scottish author Samuel Smiles (1812–1904), *Self-Help: with Illustrations of Character, Conduct, and Perseverance*, published in London in 1859 and revised in 1866, was translated into Arabic by Ya'qub Sarruf under the title *Kitab sirr al-najah*, *The Secret of Success*. First published in Beirut in 1880 and Cairo in 1886, the Arabic translation became required reading at Christian missionary schools in Lebanon. Ya'qub Sarruf (1852–1927) was a graduate of the Syrian Protestant College (the future American University) in Beirut, a prolific intellectual and co-editor of the influential journal *al-Muqtataf*. Jurji Zaydan (1861–1914), the famous journalist and man of letters, who had formerly been close to Sarruf, was deeply impressed by Smiles' concept of self-help. The Egyptian Khedive Isma'il was familiar with it. The Egyptian nationalist Mustafa Kamil (1874–1908) adopted the motto of self-help for a school he founded in 1898, underscoring the close connection between self-help and education. Smiles defined as his task:[21]

> to stimulate youths to apply themselves diligently to right pursuits, – sparing neither labour, pains, nor self-denial in prosecuting them, – and to rely upon their own efforts in life, rather than depend upon the help or patronage of others, it will also be found, from the examples given ... that the duty of helping one's self in the highest sense involves the helping of one's neighbours.

Hasan al-Banna breathed the same spirit. He preached the ethics of work, thrift, temperance and discipline, and he also lived it. He was driven, serious, devoted and completely focused on his goal. As a trained clockmaker and schoolteacher, he was used to imposing order on himself and others; his *Letters* and *Memoirs* constantly account for time and money spent. To acquire those habits, he did not have to rely on books and the type of education he received at Egyptian government schools, which strongly insisted on order and industry: his father must have served as a model of productive discipline, as patience and precision were required for all his occupations, repairing watches, binding books and re-arranging Hadith. Did Hasan al-Banna therefore acquire a specifically modern sense of time and time management? No doubt. And yet to say that it is specifically modern is not to imply that it has no antecedents in the Islamic tradition. In an article published in June 1946, al-Banna argued that time is not just money, as the materialists have it, but that "time is life" (*al-waqt huwa l-hayat*), referring to the Muslim ascetic al-Hasan al-Basri (d. 110/728) as an eminent advocate of this maxim.[22]

There was at any rate no place for leisure and entertainment in his programme for reform, unless it was useful entertainment, showing Muslim audiences the path to proper conduct. The primary role of poetry, drama, journalism and the theatre was to edify – not to serve as a pretext for idleness and diversion. "Diversion," in fact, was exactly what made entertainment so objectionable, because it "diverted" Muslims from the straight path. Al-Banna and the Muslim Brothers did approve of "Islamic" poetry and plays, which incidentally were mostly read and only rarely staged.[23] In a similar vein, higher cadres were urged to speak *fusha*, literary Arabic, not the Egyptian dialect. Given the strong concern of the Arab renaissance, *nahda*, and the Salafiyya with the revival of the Arabic language and given his own profession as a teacher of Arabic, his interest in fostering the Arabic language is not surprising.

Al-Banna's tract *Risalat al-Ta'alim*, written for the Battalions in the late 1930s, conveys the kind of mentality and behaviour he wished to instil in Muslim youth. Al-Banna insisted that they be manly and virtuous, industrious and temperate, cleanly and punctual, strong and self-confident, modest and polite, physically fit and spiritually aware. They must be active and productive, willing to help others; they must be careful with time and take daily stock of their activities; engage in daily recitations of the Qur'an, Hadiths and special devotions (*wird*), adopt Islamic modes of dress, speech, food and furniture, and buy only goods made in Egypt; they must partake of tea and coffee only in moderate quantities, they must not sit around in coffeehouses, and entirely refrain from smoking; they must always speak the truth, keep their promises, admit to error and be fair, tolerant and gentle with others. At the same time, and this marks al-Banna as the government employee he was, they must be willing to enter government service.

What also transpires is the decidedly masculine streak in his vision of New Muslim Man (and the word has been chosen with care): like many modern reformers, Samuel Smiles included, Hasan al-Banna firmly believed that great men make history. Muslim youth required role models like the *mujahidun* of the early Islamic period. They needed to be told heroic stories to inspire them to similar acts of heroism. Women figure only on the margins, as helpers of men.

With regard to women's rights, Hasan al-Banna was possibly even more conservative than many of his followers: he firmly opposed any ideas of female liberation or emancipation and endorsed the principle of male superiority and guardianship over women (*qiwama*, referring to Q 4:34).[24] Women's natural sphere was the home and family, and social intercourse with men was to be reduced to a minimum. Women were not to leave the house to go out to work or school unless absolutely necessary; modest dress including the headscarf was mandatory. Al-Banna denied women access to leading positions in society as well as in his Society as unbefitting their sex and nature; thus they were to be barred from the legal profession, parliament and government, and they were not to be admitted as witnesses in court. To assess this position, one must of course take into account attitudes across Egyptian society to gender, female education and women in the public sphere. Still, al-Banna was even more conservative than Shaykh al-Azhar Mustafa al-Maraghi, whom he publicly criticized for his lenient position on certain gender issues.

Hasan al-Banna's vision of New Islamic Man corresponded perfectly with what Timothy Mitchell and other critics of Western modernity have described as the ultimate objective of modern schooling, in Europe as well as in the Middle East: to transform the individual into an object to be put to work for the sake of a grander scheme. "To change the tastes and habits of an entire people," Mitchell noted, "politics had to seize upon the individual, and by a new means of education make him or her into a modern political subject – frugal, innocent and, above all, busy" (*Colonising Egypt*, p. 75). Very true – but here we have the colonial project transformed into a decidedly anti-colonial programme of Islamic empowerment, re-forming the Muslim as pious believer and self-confident citizen of the Islamic commonwealth.

THE VIRTUOUS CITY

Among the various elements of his thought, it is al-Banna's political views that have been studied most thoroughly by scholars, critics and admirers alike.[25] Again it is necessary to place them in context so as to avoid the exceptionalism characteristic of much writing on Islam and Islamism. The basics can be easily summed up: Islam charges believers with heavy responsibilities, but it also gives them unalienable rights that are relevant to politics, reflecting the dual notion of the Arabic word *haqq* as both right and duty. The state has a crucial function in the Islamic project and a clear mission, that is, to implement the Islamic way of life, or the Islamic order, based on the Shari'a. However, al-Banna believed that in Islam government is not divorced from the community or the people, and the ruler is not omnipotent. Like any other human being, he is subject to divine law and he has to practise consultation (*shura*). Muslims must not submit to unjust rule, especially if it is exerted by infidels; according to the well-known Muslim Brother motto, "The Qur'an is our constitution, the Prophet is our leader" (using the term *za'im* at a time when political leaders in the Arab world were commonly addressed as such).

Islam thus acts as the most potent source of empowerment. In Brynjar Lia's words, belief in the comprehensiveness of Islam represented a "liberation," confirming that a Muslim "by virtue of his adherence to Islam, has the right to have a voice in all aspects concerning the nation" (*Society*, p. 202). In a speech he gave to the Muslim Brother Student Section in 1938, al-Banna declared "emphatically, clearly and openly" that Islam was not what its enemies wished to reduce it to. Rather, "it is faith and devotion, homeland and nationality, tolerance and power, ethics and matter, culture and law. If a Muslim desires the rule of [his] Islam, he must concern himself with all affairs of his nation. He who does not concern himself with the affairs of the Muslims does not belong to them." A Muslim, he continued, will not live Islam completely unless he engages in politics (*Ila l-tullab*, pp. 9f.). Did this conviction comprise a concept of civil society? It would seem so, given al-Banna's early involvement in voluntary associations and the activities of the Society of the Muslim Brothers, although the terms *mujtama' madani* or *mujtama' ahli* that are today used to describe a "civil society" were not yet in vogue in his time.

According to al-Banna, Islam offers firm guidelines on how to organize government, define its rights and duties, provide for its control and supervision, and detail the conditions of obedience to it. These guidelines allow for popular sovereignty and the accountability of the ruler(s) within the framework of Islam. In line with his emphasis on individual "morals" and "character," al-Banna put great emphasis on individual rights and responsibilities. But he also charged the (Islamic) state with wide-ranging tasks and functions to regulate the affairs of the community, ensure social justice and exert moral control. It cannot be a coincidence that he was himself a government employee who had received virtually all his education in government schools.

If some Muslim Brothers harboured dreams of a just tyrant (*al-mustabidd al-'adil*), they remained a minority. Hasan al-Banna advocated constitutional consultative rule (*hukm dusturi shurawi*), based on consultation, *shura*, and a written constitution. Although he was basically against hereditary rule, he did not oppose the ruling dynasty in Egypt and King Faruq more particularly. In his speech to the Fifth General Conference in 1939, al-Banna explained that the principles of constitutional government corresponded perfectly to the teachings of Islam. For this reason, the Muslim Brothers considered that of all the existing systems of government, the constitutional one came closest to Islam, and that they would not exchange it for any other system (*Rasa'il*, p. 172).

To define the elements of Islamic government in specific detail was clearly not seen as urgent – not to mention the fact that it would carry the seed of conflict, running against his basic impulse to focus on what unites Muslims, not what divides them. The one exception was his critique of parties and partisanship, *al-hizbiyya*. Politics, al-Banna insisted, was an integral part of Islam which did not recognize any distinction between religion and politics. But politics was not party politics. Though multi-partyism might possibly be viable in certain countries, it was not suitable for Egypt, which needed only one thing: unity of rank and purpose. As mentioned before, al-Banna was not alone among his contemporaries in criticizing the disintegration of party politics and the machinations of party politicians. The *Black Book* published by Makram 'Ubayd in 1943, when he split from the Wafd Party, exposing the corruption rampant in Wafdist ranks, is the most famous example. To replace the existing parties, Hasan al-Banna advocated a national body (*hay'a wataniyya*) composed of delegates of all societal groups and associations, as well as experts and specialists in various fields.

Al-Banna also propagated what he and others called the "application of the Shari'a." Religion was the moral foundation of the nation, and the Qur'an, the Muslim Brothers proclaimed, was its constitution. By the same token, the Shari'a served as the prime symbol of moral integrity, cultural authenticity and national independence. It was the link between Islamic law and national self-determination that made al-Banna's call attractive to a larger Egyptian audience.

Islamic law was widely understood to be divine law, removed from human manipulation, the ultimate arbiter of everything. At the same time, it could be presented as national law and its application as the supreme expression of national self-determination. It could also be invoked as a moral code to "guide," censure and correct the ruling classes and their imitation of foreign models. The difficulty lay in its actual implementation in twentieth-century Egypt.

Like other Muslim reformers before and after him, al-Banna described Islamic law as both eternal and flexible, adaptable to the ever-changing circumstances of time and place. Like 'Abduh and Rida before him, he emphasized the "ease" (*yusr*) and flexibility of Islam, its broad outlines and general principles, *kulliyyat* and *maqasid*, at the expense of petty detail, *juz'iyyat*. It is true that he did occasionally write on matters of ritual, including Sufi *dhikr*, and published what were called fatwas on a number of issues, from female dress to the permissibility of reciting the Qur'an on the radio.[26] But in line with his effort to promote unity, not dissension, he avoided controversial issues, for this would have entailed thinking systematically about Islamic jurisprudence, *fiqh*, for which he lacked both time and the required training. Al-Banna recognized that *fiqh* had always been plural, as expressed in the several legal schools, or *madhahib*, which in themselves were never monolithic, and that it had the potential for divisiveness. He was also aware that Egyptian audiences were perhaps in favour of following Shari'a in general, but that the canonical punishments, *hudud*, were widely thought to be obsolete. The *hudud*, he repeatedly stated, were an integral part of Islam and perfectly reconcilable with modern legal concepts, whatever that meant exactly.

One thing was clear, however: moral control had to be firmly secured, and the cultural field, including notably the media and press, had to be closely supervised to ensure that it remained within the bounds of Islam. His tract *To the Light* (1947) furnishes a comprehensive list of how to purify culture and society. One American scholar was reminded of an "updated Salem," the epitome of puritan rigour in seventeenth-century New England.[27] The Muslim Brothers were not alone in advocating such stringent measures, but in the 1930s and 1940s they did not represent mainstream opinion. With regard to its cultural and economic values, the Wafd, for instance, was liberal; so were the Liberal Constitutionalists. The Muslim Brothers decidedly were not. To Hasan al-Banna, liberal amounted to libertarian, that is to say to having no morals at all. What he stood for was a profoundly moral order.

A MORAL ECONOMY

Hasan al-Banna always showed a marked concern for social issues, even though until the mid-1940s the Muslim Brothers did not elaborate a programme of social and economic reform that went beyond the conveniently broad ideals of social justice, equity and (national) economic independence. To this end, he encouraged individual thrift, industry, economy and temperance and at the same time invited state protection and intervention to eradicate poverty, unemployment, illiteracy and disease. His profound belief in the necessity of unity also affected his socio-economic ideas: Egypt was to be one nation undivided, thriving on the cooperation of all social groups and classes. Thus he propagated the ideal of social harmony, not class struggle; anti-communism was a pillar of his world view. Hasan al-Banna was acutely sensitive to questions of wealth and status, and he was well qualified to speak on the subject: not only did he come from a rural family of moderate means, he also travelled widely in the country, visiting towns, villages and country estates. Already as a young teacher in Isma'iliyya he had censured the Egyptian upper class. An article published in *al-Nadhir* in 1939 exemplifies the moral tone of his critique:[28]

> This class among whom you will find the rulers who have made the rule of this country a private matter for themselves, this class will be our arch enemy, because our Islamic mission restricts their avidity, puts an end to their greed and opens the eyes of the people to their evil deeds and disgraceful acts.

There was nothing original in his critique of large landowners facing a miserable mass of peasants, afflicted by poverty, ignorance and disease, especially in the late 1930s and the 1940s. In response to a Wafdist who, in 1939, had defended the existing class system in terms of Islam, Hasan al-Banna rejoined that, on the contrary, Islam preferred nobody on the grounds of blood, race, descent, poverty or wealth. According to Islam everyone was equal. Islam did *not* approve of the class system.[29] This is, of course, a classic expression of egalitarianism in Islam, which has indeed a strong tradition. In Friday prayer, al-Banna saw a community united, with no visible social distinctions, aligned in perfect order, hearing the word of truth. Similarly, during the pilgrimage to Mecca, the pilgrim's cloth, *ihram*, served as a sign of equality, symbolizing the unity and brotherhood of humankind. However, as is well known, Islamic egalitarianism as understood by al-Banna needs to be qualified with regard to gender and religion. He refrained from going deeper into the matter.

When it comes to the means of socio-economic change, we once again note the characteristic blend of Islamic and modern references. In line with Islamic law, al-Banna opposed interest (*riba*), and the Islamic alms tax, *zakat*, was to serve as an important instrument to achieve social justice. At the moral level, he attacked the pervading spirit of materialism and consumerism:[30]

> Have the Muslims understood the Book of their Lord in this fashion, so that their souls have been uplifted and their spirits raised on high? So that they have freed themselves from the bondage of matter, and purified themselves of the pleasures of fleshly lusts and cravings? ... Or are they prisoners of their lusts and slaves of their cravings and desires, whose sole interest is a delicate mouthful, a fast car, a handsome suit, a cosy nap, a fair wife, a false appearance and a vain title?

But al-Banna also saw the modern state as a major player in the national economy. In the 1940s, demands became more specific, moving beyond the general principles of moral uplift and individual reform: the Muslim Brothers called for government reorganization, pay raises, social welfare policies, nationalization, the establishment of public enterprises (a concern of Egyptian nationalists since the 1920s), a reform of taxation, imposition of the *zakat*, labour legislation, cooperatives in the countryside, modern farming methods, the introduction of an Islamic banking system, etc. These demands tied in well with their concern for education and the fight against illiteracy. In his speech at the Sixth General Conference in 1941, Hasan al-Banna put heavy emphasis on the need to replace foreign domination and economic control with nationally owned enterprises. Yet he never proposed radical structural reform, such as a comprehensive agrarian reform, or any encroachment on private property (except for foreign-owned). It would seem that this reluctance to challenge the system reflected the interests of the Muslim Brothers themselves, many of whom owned land; al-Banna himself was a prime exponent of this class. What he focused on was foreign domination and what he saw as exploitation by the Jews, phenomena inextricably linked to the sense of national humiliation and inferiority. Yet he never really developed the theme. After his death, others like Muhammad al-Ghazali, Sayyid Qutb and his younger brother Jamal were to go much further in their critique of the socio-economic order.

A CHARISMATIC COMMUNITY?

Was the Muslim Brotherhood a "charismatic community"? Witnesses testify to Hasan al-Banna's charisma and his pivotal role in the Brotherhood. Among the Brothers, al-Banna was consciously portrayed as a role model, and anecdotes were told about him to inspire the Brothers. The Muslim Brotherhood was not a one-man show, but Hasan al-Banna was beyond a doubt its most prominent public face. In 1944, a British embassy report remarked with regard to the Muslim Brotherhood:[31]

> Its weakness, however, lies in its leadership. Hassan el Banna is not only the undisputed leader of the Brotherhood but he is its only outstanding personality. The society is completely dependent on him,

> and although he may be dangerous because the power he can wield the dependence of the Brotherhood on his leadership may yet be the cause of its downfall ... should Hassan el Banna for any reason be removed, the Ikhwan, in the absence of any successor of comparable driving force and inspiration, might easily crumble away.

A number of elements merit consideration in this context: the oath of allegiance; the title of *murshid*; the teaching methods and teaching materials studied and memorized by the Muslim Brothers; the selection of leading cadres, decision-making processes and the negotiation of conflict. The oath of allegiance (*bay'a*) given by the Muslim Brothers was modelled on early Muslim practice when the community had paid homage to the Rightly Guided Caliphs, who were the successors to the Prophet. The oath could also be seen in the light of Sufi practices binding the Sufi aspirant to his master, and it was introduced into the Brotherhood from the very beginning. But there was also protest against what some Muslim Brothers saw as unlawful veneration, or worship even, of a human being coming dangerously close to *shirk*, idolatry, reflecting earlier criticism al-Banna had had to face in Isma'iliyya.[32] Here social class came into play: at least in the early 1930s, some local notables refused to take an oath of allegiance to a schoolteacher who was their social inferior. The conflict was resolved by taking the oath together, rather than to Hasan al-Banna. At the Second General Conference in 1934, a written oath of allegiance was made mandatory for all registered members, detailed in article 6 of the General Law. This was still a pledge of mutual solidarity among brothers, a "contract with God" rather than an oath of loyalty and (blind) obedience towards Hasan al-Banna.

Still, the term *bay'a* suggests an unequal relationship, reflecting the concept of *wala'* with its broad semantic field, which ranges from loyalty to patronage. At the Third General Conference held in March 1935, members reportedly swore complete obedience to the General Guide (*al-sam' wa-l-ta'a*). At the same time, Hasan al-Banna's tract *On Obedience* (*Risalat al-Ta'a*) was distributed among members. Yet as further developments were to show, blind obedience was by no means assured. The very emphasis on obedience and the closing of ranks (not least to prevent repressive measures brought against the Society as a whole if, in opposition to express orders, individual members were to act "rashly") suggests that all was not well. It is also worthy of mention that the Muslim Sisters did not swear obedience in the way their male counterparts did.

What might be called the "politics of address" equally merits attention. Which title – *ustadh*, *efendi*, *murshid*, *shaykh*, *imam* – was used when and by whom? The most significant title here is *al-murshid al-'amm*, a title commonly translated as General or Supreme Guide, and of course linked to the concept of guidance, *irshad*. The title is best known from the Sufi tradition, where it designates a spiritual master, although Rashid Rida used it for the preachers to be trained at his Dar al-Da'wa wa-l-Irshad. The choice expresses a conscious avoidance of "worldly" titles with a claim to power, like *ra'is* or *za'im*, which were applied to contemporary political leaders, such as Sa'd Zaghlul or Mustafa al-Nahhas; according to the Muslim Brothers, only the Prophet was their *za'im*. Hasan al-Banna first used the title of General Guide in September 1932, after the conflict over his leadership of the Society of the Muslim Brothers had been more or less resolved. In 1934 it was officially conferred upon him (Lia, *Society*, pp. 98, 116f.).

Hasan al-Banna was widely described as the "architect" (*muhandis*) of the Muslim Brotherhood. The designation also referred to the ideological "construction" (training, education, formation, indoctrination) of its members provided by Hasan al-Banna through his tracts, editorials and articles. Many of them were required reading, ideally to be memorized by ordinary members and advanced cadres alike, and many actually were memorized by devoted Brothers. As has been mentioned, some were later supplemented with commentaries (*sharh*); no text written by another Muslim Brother acquired similar status. At the Second General Conference in 1934, Hasan al-Banna was given a mandate to formulate a set of principles to be studied by all members, and preachers were to be appointed by the General Guidance Office to act as a kind of instructor to members (one cannot help thinking of a *politkommissar*). *Our Creed* (*'Aqidatuna*), a short tract containing ten articles written by Hasan al-Banna, had to be memorized by all members; higher cadres also had to study commentaries on *'Aqidatuna*.

The mechanisms designed to mediate and resolve internal conflict have not been studied well. According to al-Banna himself, leadership was entirely based on merit; it was a burden, and it demanded sacrifice. On more than one occasion he asked the Brothers whether they were ready to share the burden with him and to commit themselves unconditionally to the mission. In spite of this rhetoric of responsibility, there are strong indications that Hasan al-Banna trusted no one and had no confidence in his fellow Muslim Brothers. At one point he noted that Ahmad al-Sukkari's heart was filled with dreams, and Hamid 'Askariyya had his own methods, and looked at him as a brother and was not willing subordinate himself. This made it difficult to "unify the thinking" (*tawhid al-fikra*) (*Memoirs*, pp. 135–7). As future developments were to show, "the thinking" was indeed never unified, and yet Hasan al-Banna remained a central reference for Muslim Brothers and other Islamists in Egypt and beyond.

CONCLUDING REMARKS

The death of Hasan al-Banna threw the Muslim Brothers into profound disarray. Members would later remember how they lost their "light" and "pole" when the charismatic *murshid* was taken from them.[33] Existing conflict within the Brotherhood came to the fore, with one faction being headed by the al-Banna family, another by leaders of the Special Apparatus. Only in October 1951 was the former judge Hasan al-Hudaybi (1891–1973) elected as the new general guide. He represented an older generation and a different social milieu from Hasan al-Banna. Youth would never guide the Muslim Brotherhood again. At the trial of the so-called Jeep Case in 1950–1, the Society of the Muslim Brothers was acquitted of responsibility for any acts of terrorism; al-Banna's assassins were tried in

1954, after the Free Officer Revolution of July 1952, and four of the defendants were given heavy sentences. In the ensuing power struggle with the Free Officers, however, the Muslim Brothers, like all autonomous political forces in the country, were ruthlessly suppressed. After Nasser's death in 1970, his successor Anwar al-Sadat ended the great *mihna*, in which thousands of Muslim Brothers and other critics of the regime had been interned, tortured or driven into exile; some, like Sayyid Qutb, who was executed in 1966, died as "martyrs" to their cause. Yet Hasan al-Banna's prediction that though the organization be outlawed and its property seized, the Muslim Brotherhood would not be destroyed and its message not extinguished, proved true. Sixty years after his death, the Muslim Brotherhood is still illegal in Egypt. But it exists, and it still invokes his legacy.

ENDNOTES

CHAPTER 1

1 Cromer, *Modern Egypt*, pp. 872–86; Reid, *Cairo University*, pp. 18f.; Steppat, *Tradition*, pp. 68ff.; see also Brown, *Peasant Politics*, pp. 59–82; *Census of 1907*, Village Tables. The narrative is based on *Letters*; al-Hajjaji, *Ruh*, pp. 75–97 offers some additional detail.
2 Eccel, *Egypt*, p. 140; Steppat, *Tradition*, p. 120; Starrett, *Putting Islam to Work*, p. 29.
3 *Letters*, pp. 20f.; *Memoirs*, p. 20; al-Jundi, *Hasan al-Banna*, pp. 163, 169; Padwick, *Muslim Devotions*; for Zarruq, see Kugle, *Rebel*.
4 De Jong, *Turuq*, esp. pp. 101–3, 107f.; Knysh, *Islamic Mysticism*, pp. 207ff.; *Memoirs*, pp. 19–29. Though "Hisafiyya" is probably correct, and used by de Jong, I have opted for Hasafiyya as the most commonly used pronunciation.
5 Heather Sharkey suggests that she was Florence Lillian White, who worked for the American Presbyterian mission in the Delta from 1919 to the mid-1920s: *American Evangelicals*, pp. 107f.
6 *Rasa'il*, p. 138; Wendell, *Five Tracts*, p. 28; for background information, see van Nieuwkerk, *Trade*, esp. pp. 38, 45–9; Armbrust, *Mass Culture*, pp. 63ff.; Baraka, *Egyptian Upper Class*, pp. 120–9; Badran, *Feminists*, pp. 192–206; Baron, *Egypt as a Woman*, pp. 50–6, 197–9.
7 *Memoirs*, pp. 55–8, 61f.; *Letters*, pp. 29f.; al-Kumi, *al-Sihafa*, pp. 100–4; Baron, *Women's Awakening*, pp. 28f.; Kramer, *Islam Assembled*, pp. 89f.; Sha'ir, *Wasa'il*, pp. 190–8; Haydar, *Adwa'*, pp. 30f.; Mayeur-Jaouen, "Les débuts".

CHAPTER 2

1 *Memoirs*, pp. 58–61, 74f.; *Letters*, pp. 101ff., 116, 119.
2 *Letters*, pp. 93f.; *Memoirs*, pp. 130, 138f.; also 'Abd al-Halim, *al-Ikhwan*, 1, p. 68.

3 Lia, *Society*, pp. 181–6; Deeb, *Party Politics*, pp. 11f., 315ff.; Ryzova, *L'effendiyya*; 'Abd al-Baqi, *Tabaqat al-afandiyya*; also Mitchell, *Society*, pp. 12f.; Kupferschmidt, "The Muslim Brothers", pp. 159f.
4 *Memoirs*, pp. 150f., 164f.; 'Abd al-Halim, *al-Ikhwan*, 1, pp. 252–6; Amin, *al-Ikhwan*, 3, pp. 165–207; Baron, *Egypt as a Woman*, pp. 209f.; Mitchell, *Society*, p. 175.
5 'Abd al-Halim, *al-Ikhwan*, 1, p. 73; *Memoirs*, pp. 162f.; Lia, *Society*, pp. 164, 182–5.
6 Glaß, *Muqtataf*, 1, pp. 40ff., 115, 164; *Memoirs*, pp. 143f.; 'Abd al-Halim, *al-Ikhwan*, 1, pp. 75, 183–5; Sha'ir, *Wasa'il*, pp. 163, 204–17.
7 Lia, *Society*, provides the best data to date; see esp. appendices I and V; also *Memoirs*, pp. 99–101 and, for British estimates, *IMAW*, 3, pp. 160, 163.
8 *Memoirs*, p. 233; Lia, *Society*, p. 231.
9 *Memoirs*, pp. 151f., 156f.; Carter, "On Spreading the Gospel"; Costet-Tardieu, *Un réformiste*, pp. 12f., 86–95; Sharkey, *American Evangelicals*, ch. 4. Amin, *al-Ikhwan*, 3, pp. 54–104 offers extensive coverage of Muslim Brother activities; Na'im, *al-Judhur*, is strongly biased.

CHAPTER 3

1 FO 371/19980, in: *IMAW*, 3, pp. 160, 163; *Memoirs*, pp. 202–7; Lia, *Society*, pp. 154–9, 237. For foreign branches, see Amin, *al-Ikhwan*, 3, pp. 353–79 (378).
2 *Memoirs*, pp. 211–20, 228ff.; Amin, *al-Ikhwan*, 3, pp. 380–479; Krämer, *Jews*, pp. 145–54; Lia, *Society*, pp. 164, 236ff., 240ff.; Gershoni and Jankowski, *Redefining*, pp. 167–91.
3 *Ila ay shay' nad'u l-nas*, in: *Rasa'il*, p. 35; Wendell, *Five Tracts*, p. 75; Lia, *Society*, p. 88 n. 37.
4 *Memoirs*, pp. 144ff.; Sha'ir, *Wasa'il*, pp. 218–29; al-Sisi, *Fi qafila*, 1, p. 54.
5 *Memoirs*, pp. 254f.; Sha'ir, *Wasa'il*, pp. 230–6.
6 Jankowski, *Egypt's Young Rebels*, pp. 5, 24f., 34f.; Deeb, *Party Politics*, pp. 75–85, 351–4, 376.
7 *Memoirs*, pp. 196, 238, 246f.; Lia, *Society*, pp. 100–2, 166–78, 220–3; *Nahwa l-nur*, in: *Rasa'il*, pp. 65f.; Wendell, *Five Tracts*, pp. 114f.; 'Abd al-Halim, *al-Ikhwan*, 1, pp. 161–8; al-Sisi, *Fi qafila*, 1, pp. 52f., 62–4.

For British perceptions of the Rovers as modelled on the Nazi SS and SA units, see *IMAW*, 3, pp. 373f. (24 December 1942).

8 *Risalat al-Ta'alim*, in: *Rasa'il*, pp. 266ff., 274; 'Abd al-Halim, *al-Ikhwan*, 1, pp. 150–60; Mitchell, *Society*, pp. 196–8, 202f.; Lia, *Society*, pp. 161f., 168–75.

9 Kramer, *Islam Assembled*, pp. 86–105; Gershoni and Jankowski, *Redefining*, pp. 145–66.

10 Quoted from Lia, *Society*, p. 217, also ibid., pp. 214–23; Amin, *al-Ikhwan*, 3, pp. 48–53.

11 Lia, *Society*, pp. 139f., 179f., 220–3, 260ff.; Haykal, *Mudhakkirat*, 2, pp. 177f.; a British secret report dated 24 December 1942 tells a slightly different story: *IMAW*, 3, pp. 374f.; *Letters*, pp. 131–7; al-Sisi, *Fi qafila*, 1, pp. 85f.

12 Mitchell, *Society*, pp. 22–5, 28f.; Lia, *Society*, pp. 154, 200, 208ff., 222f., 263–8; al-Sisi, *Fi qafila*, pp. 1, 83–7; *IMAW*, 3, pp. 361ff., 374f. For Axis sympathies and propaganda, see Krämer, *Jews*, pp. 154ff.

13 Lia, *Society*, pp. 268f.; *IMAW*, 3, pp. 376f., 391, 397f.; 'Abd al-Halim, *al-Ikhwan*, 1, pp. 294–9, 324–32; al-Sisi, *Fi qafila*, 1, pp. 93–5.

14 Zaki, *al-Ikhwan*, pp. 185–99; Amin, *al-Ikhwan*, 3, pp. 165ff.; Baron, *Egypt as a Woman*, pp. 189–213; Mitchell, *Society*, p. 175.

15 Lia, *Society*, pp. 151–4, 200, 208–14 and appendix 1; al-Sisi, *Fi qafila*, 1, pp. 139, 190; for British estimates, see *IMAW*, 3, pp. 378, 389, 396f.

16 In addition to Mitchell, *Society*, see Lia, *Society*, pp. 251–3, 262f.; Jankowski, *Egypt's Young Rebels*, p. 40.

17 *Rasa'il*, pp. 147–87; Mitchell, *Society*, pp. 18f.; Lia, *Society*, pp. 178f., 247–56.

18 Mitchell, *Society*, pp. 200–8 (205); also Jankowski, *Egypt's Young Rebels*, p. 82; Shadi, *Safahat*, pp. 84ff.

19 Mitchell, *Society*, p. 26; Lia, *Society*, pp. 134, 145, 186–90.

20 Mitchell, *Society*, pp. 52–5; 'Abd al-Halim, *al-Ikhwan*, 1, pp. 269–76, 456ff.; *IMAW*, 3, pp. 364, 374, 390; al-Sisi, *Fi qafila*, 1, pp. 150–66.

21 *Ahadith al-jum'a*, pp. 142ff., 152, 156f.; al-Sisi, *Fi qafila*, 1, p. 246; Mitchell, *Society*, pp. 55–79; Abdalla, *Student Movement*, pp. 62–79; Krämer, *Jews*, pp. 208–19.

22 Douglas, *Free Yemeni Movement*; 'Abd al-Halim, *al-Ikhwan*, 1, pp. 399–408; al-Sisi, *Fi qafila*, 1, pp. 204–7.

23 Mitchell, *Society*, p. 62; Abu Ghadir, *Qadiyyatuna*; al-Sisi, *Fi qafila*, 1, pp. 258f.; Shadi, *Safahat*, pp. 54–6.
24 Mitchell, *Society*, pp. 63–5, 74–6; Krämer, *Jews*, pp. 211ff.; al-Sisi, *Fi qafila*, 1, pp. 269–75.
25 *Ahadith al-jum'a*, pp. 312–14 (3 December 1948) and 105–7 (19 December 1946).
26 Mitchell, *Society*, pp. 65–79, 203–8; 'Abd al-Halim, *al-Ikhwan*, 2, pp. 22–30; Shadi, *Safahat*, pp. 337–46; al-Sisi, *Hasan al-Banna*, pp. 283–6.
27 Abu Ghadir, *Qadiyyatuna*; 'Abd al-Halim, *al-Ikhwan*, 2, pp. 46–59, 387–91; Shadi, *Safahat*, pp. 60–8; Salim, *al-Bulis*, p. 326. For torture, see al-Sisi, *Fi qafila*, 1, pp. 297–9. Under presidents Sadat and Mubarak, a large body of Muslim Brother literature describing torture in Nasserist prisons appeared.
28 Al-Jundi, *Hasan al-Banna*, pp. 278–97, 539; al-Sisi, *Fi qafila*, 1, pp. 290f.; *Letters*, pp. 8, 36, 48f., 73–6.

CHAPTER 4

1 Lia, *Society*, pp. 21, 36; *Memoirs*, p. 13; for the diary, see *Letters*, p. 86.
2 Deeb, *Party Politics*, pp. 162f.; Brown, *Peasant Politics*, p. 167; Baraka, *Egyptian Upper Class*, pp. 22–46, 212–15.
3 *Memoirs*, pp. 30, 52f.; *Letters*, pp. 97, 113f. See also his position on hats and turbans in *al-Fiqh wa-l-fatawa*, pp. 257–66.
4 Al-Bishri, *al-Haraka*, preface, pp. 42ff.; al-Nafisi, *al-Haraka*; for al-Banna, see, e.g., *Rasa'il*, pp. 31, 40; *Risalat al-mu'tamar al-sadis*.
5 Lia, *Society*, p. 83; Mitchell, *Society*, p. 230; *Rasa'il*, esp. pp. 27f.
6 The best study to date is Sharkey, *American Evangelicals*; see esp. ch. 1 and pp. 1, 32f., 63, 73–8 for estimated figures of converts, and pp. 124–33 for Muslim orphans and Christian conversion; al-Na'im, *al-Judhur* and Amin, *al-Ikhwan* illustrate the fervour of Muslim anti-missionary sentiment.
7 *Memoirs*, esp. pp. 19–27; *al-Fiqh wa-l-fatawa*, pp. 31–3, 158–69, 209–18, 234–41; al-Sisi, *Fi qafila*, 1, pp. 28f., 42; Mitchell, *Society*, pp. 214–6; Lia, *Society*, pp. 38, 114–17.
8 *Rasa'il*, p. 26; Wendell, *Five Tracts*, pp. 61f.; also *Ahadith al-jum'a*, p. 96; Lübben, "Träume", pp. 36ff. For the concept of "Easternism," variously

defined, see Gershoni and Jankowski, *Egypt*, pp. 255–69, and Gershoni and Jankowski, *Redefining*, pp. 35–53.

9 *Rasa'il*, p. 140; Wendell, *Five Tracts*, p. 30; similarly the short tract *Our Creed*, *'Aqidatuna* (e.g., in 'Abd al-Halim, *al-Ikhwan*, 1, pp. 40f.) or *Ahadith al-jum'a*, pp. 243–5, 263 (January and February 1948).

10 *Rasa'il*, pp. 32f.; Wendell, *Five Tracts*, p. 71; see also *Rasa'il*, pp. 38, 40–2; Wendell, *Five Tracts*, pp. 78, 80f., 84.

11 *Rasa'il*, p. 14; Wendell, *Five Tracts*, p. 44; for the broader context, see Brown, *Peasant Politics*, p. 62.

12 *Ahadith al-jum'a*, p. 129 (13 February 1947); similarly, pp. 25f.; Wendell, *Five Tracts*, pp. 60–2.

13 For various practices and understandings of *jihad*, see notably Bonner, *Jihad*; Cook, *Understanding Jihad*, and, by the same author, *Martyrdom in Islam*.

14 *Rasa'il*, pp. 63–5; Wendell, *Five Tracts*, pp. 110–13; but see also the collection of articles dating from 1948, published under the title of *Peace in Islam* (*al-Salam fi l-islam*).

15 *Rasa'il*, p. 261; Wendell, *Five Tracts*, p. 151. See similarly *Ahadith al-jum'a*, p. 152 (16 May 1947); *al-Salam fi l-islam*.

16 *Ahadith al-jum'a*, pp. 62–4, 185f.; Mitchell, *Society*, pp. 207f.; Smith, "Crisis"; Gershoni and Jankowski, *Redefining*, pp. 54–78.

17 *Rasa'il*, p. 33; Wendell, *Five Tracts*, p. 71. See similarly *Rasa'il*, pp. 9, 41f., 49f., 62f.; Wendell, *Five Tracts*, pp. 50, 82f., 92f.

18 For racism, see *Da'watuna*, in: *Rasa'il*, pp. 21f.; Wendell, *Five Tracts*, pp. 54f.; Lia, *Society*, p. 80; *Da'watuna fi tawr jadid*, in: Sha'ir, *Wasa'il*, pp. 559–62; for unity, see, e.g., *Ahadith al-jum'a*, pp. 40–57, 96–9, 121–3.

19 Quoted with slight corrections from Lia, *Society*, p. 79; see also *Rasa'il*, pp. 17, 19, 50, 62f.; Wendell, *Five Tracts*, pp. 48, 50f., 94f., 110; *Ahadith al-jum'a*, pp. 11, 40–3, 140. For contemporary intellectual trends, see Gershoni and Jankowski, *Redefining*, esp. pp. 79–96.

20 See, e.g., *Da'watuna*, in: *Rasa'il*, p. 17; Wendell, *Five Tracts*, p. 48; *Ahadith al-jum'a*, pp. 79–82, 110–12; Glaß, *Muqtataf*, 1, p. 138, traces the sacralization of patriotism back to the journal *al-Jinan*, founded in 1870; for the status of non-Muslims, see notably *Nahwa l-nur*, in: *Rasa'il*, pp. 69ff.; Wendell, *Five Tracts*, pp. 119f.

21 Preface to the 2nd ed., London 1866, quoted from Smiles, *Self-Help*,

p. 3; see also T. Mitchell, *Colonising Egypt*, pp. 108–10; Glaß, *Muqtataf*, 1, pp. 183f., 191.

22 *Ahadith al-jum'a*, pp. 27–9; *Hadith al-thalatha'*, pp. 446–9; *al-Wasaya al-'ashar*; al-Qaradawi, *al-Waqt*; Lübben, "Träume", pp. 235f.

23 Talima, *Hasan al-Banna* and Amin, *al-Ikhwan*, 3, pp. 254–99 furnish interesting examples of "Islamic" poetry, short stories, theatre plays and even "operas" that were publicly performed.

24 Al-Banna, *al-Mar'a al-muslima; al-Fiqh wa-l-fatawa*, pp. 242–56; Amin, *al-Ikhwan*, 3, pp. 165–207.

25 Mitchell, *Society*, pp. 260ff.; Ghanim, *al-Fikr al-siyasi*; Krämer, *Gottes Staat*, pp. 182–92; among his *rasa'il*, see notably *Mushkilatuna fi daw' al-nizam al-islami*, *Nizam al-hukm* and *Ila l-tullab*.

26 *Al-Fiqh wa-l-fatawa*; see esp. *Rasa'il*, pp. 23f. (*Da'watuna*), 46 (*Ila ay shay'?*) and 269 (*al-Ta'alim*); also Mitchell, *Society*, pp. 236–41.

27 Wendell, *Five Tracts*, pp. 4 and 126–9; *Rasa'il*, pp. 74–7.

28 Quoted from Lia, *Society*, p. 211; also Baraka, *Egyptian Upper Class*, pp. 160–9; Meijer, *Quest*.

29 *Al-Nadhir*, quoted from Lia, *Society*, p. 206; for the subsequent statements, see *Ahadith al-jum'a*, pp. 10, 89–91; see further Marlow, *Hierarchy*; Krämer, "Justice"; Meijer, *Quest*.

30 *Ila ay shay'?*, in: *Rasa'il*, p. 33; Wendell, *Five Tracts*, p. 72; note the Sufi references. See also *al-Nizam al-Iqtisadi*, in: *Rasa'il*, pp. 228–45; Mitchell, *Society*, pp. 272–94.

31 FO 371/41334, Political Intelligence Committee, Paper No. 49, 25 July 1944 (in: *IMAW*, 3, p. 400); see also Lia, *Society*, pp. 69, 93ff.

32 Lia, *Society*, pp. 37, 104–6, 119f.; *Memoirs*, p. 151; see also above, pp. 30–4.

33 See, e.g., Shadi, *Safahat*, pp. 69–72; for critical voices, see al-Nafisi, *al-Haraka*; for a survey of subsequent events, see Mitchell, *Society*; Krämer, "Aus Erfahrung lernen?"

BIBLIOGRAPHY

DOCUMENTS AND ARCHIVAL MATERIALS

The Census of Egypt Taken in 1907. Cairo, National Printing Department, 1909

The Census of Egypt Taken in 1917. Cairo, Government Press, 1920

Century Census, Egypt 1882–1906. CD-ROM, Cairo, CEDEJ and CAPMAS, 2007

Egypt, Ministry of Finance. Statistical and Census Department, *Population Census of Egypt, 1937*. Cairo, Government Press, Bulaq, 1942

Islamic Movements in the Arab World, 1913–1966, ed. Anita L. P. Burdett. 4 vols. Archive Editions, 1998 (cited *IMAW*)

THE LEGACY OF AHMAD AL-BANNA (PUBLISHED WORKS)

al-Banna, Ahmad, *Bada'i' al-minan fi jam' wa-tartib musnad al-Shafi'i wa-l-sunan mudhaylan bil-qawl al-hasan sharh bada'i' al-minan*. 2 vols. Cairo, Dar al-Anwar, 1369/1950

al-Banna, Ahmad, *Tanwir al-af'ida al-zakiyya fi adillat adhkar al-wazifa al-Zarruqiyya*. Damanhur, 1330/1912

THE LEGACY OF HASAN AL-BANNA

Ahadith al-jum'a lil-imam al-shahid Hasan al-Banna, ed. and annotated by 'Isam Talima. Cairo, Dar al-Tawzi' wa-l-Nashr al-Islamiyya, 2005

Amin 'Abd al-'Aziz, Jum'a, ed., *Silsila min turath al-imam al-Banna*. Vol. 4: *al-Fiqh wa-l-fatawa*. Alexandria, Dar al-Da'wa, 2005

al-Banna, Hasan, *Mudhakkirat al-da'wa wa-l-da'iya*. Cairo, n.d., n.p. (cited *Memoirs*) al-Banna, Hasan, *Risalat al-mu'tamar al-sadis lil-ikhwan al-muslimin al-mun'aqad fi yanayir 1941m*. Al-Mansura, Dar al-Wafa', n.d.

al-Banna, Hasan, *al-Salam fi l-islam*. 2nd ed., n.p., Manshurat al-'Asr al-Hadith, 1971

al-Banna, Jamal, *Khitabat Hasan al-Banna al-shabb ila abihi*. Cairo, Dar al-Fikr, n.d. (cited *Letters*)

Diwan Sari' al-Ghawani naqqahahu wa-sahhahu wa-'alaqa 'alayhi al-ustadh al-jalil Hasan afandi Ahmad al-Banna al-mudarris bil-madaris al-amiriyya. Cairo, al-Maktaba al-'Alamiyya, n.d. (after 1932)

al-Fiqh wa-l-fatawa. Silsila min turath al-imam al-Banna, ed. Jum'a Amin 'Abd al-'Aziz. Vol. 4, Cairo, Dar al-Da'wa, 2005

Hadith al-thalatha' lil-imam Hasan al-Banna, ed. Ahmad 'Isa 'Ashur. Cairo, Maktabat al-Qur'an, n.d. (1985)

Ila l-tullab, kalimat al-imam al-shahid Hasan al-Banna fi mu'tamar talabat al-ikhwan al-muslimin al-Muharram 1357h. Alexandria, Dar al-Da'wa, n.d.

Majmu'at rasa'il al-imam al-shahid Hasan al-Banna. Cairo, Dar al-Shihab, n.d. (cited *Rasa'il*)

al-Mar'a al-muslima, ed. Muhammad Nasir al-Din al-Albani. Cairo, Dar al-Maktaba al-Salafiyya, 1983

al-Wasaya al-'ashar lil-imam al-shahid Hasan al-Banna, ed. 'Abd al-'Azim Ibrahim al-Mut'ani. Cairo, Dar al-Shuruq, 1983

Wendell, Charles, *Five Tracts of Hasan Al-Banna' (1906–1949): a Selection from Majmu'at Rasa'il al-Imam al-Shahid Hasan al-Banna'. Translated from the Arabic and annotated by Charles Wendell*. Berkeley, University of California Press, 1978

MUSLIM BROTHER WRITINGS

'Abd al-Halim, Mahmud, *al-Ikhwan al-muslimun. Ahdath sana'at al-tarikh. Ru'ya min al-dakhil*. 3 vols. Alexandria, Dar al-Da'wa, 1979, 1981, 1985

Abu Ghadir, Fahmi, ed., *Qadiyyatuna*. N.p., 1398/1978

Amin 'Abd al-'Aziz, Jum'a, *al-Ikhwan wa-l-mujtama' al-misri wa-l-dawli fi fatrat min 1928–1938m*. Cairo, Dar al-Tawzi' wa-l-Nashr al-Islamiyya, 2003 (*Awraq min tarikh al-ikhwan al-muslimin*, vol. 3)

al-Baquri, Ahmad Hasan, *Baqaya dhikrayat*. Cairo, Markaz al-Ahram, 1988
Bayyumi, Zakariya Sulayman, *al-Ikhwan al-muslimun wa-l-jama'at al-islamiyya fi l-hayat al-siyasiyya al-misriyya 1928-1948*. Cairo, Maktabat Wahba, 1979
Ghanim, Ibrahim al-Bayyumi, *al-Fikr al-siyasi lil-imam Hasan al-Banna*. Cairo, Dar al-Tawzi' wa-l-Nashr al-Islamiyya, 1992
al-Hajjaji, Ahmad Anas, *Ruh wa-rayhan*. 2nd ed., Cairo, Maktabat Wahba, 1401/1981
Hathut, Hassan, *al-'Aqd al-farid. 'Ashar sanawat ma'a l-imam Hasan al-Banna*. Cairo, Dar al-Shuruq, 2000
Hayba, Muhammad Mansur Mahmud, *al-Sihafa al-islamiyya fi misr bayna 'Abd al-Nasir wa-l-Sadat (1952–1981m)*. Al-Mansura, Dar al-Wafa', 1990
al-Jundi, Anwar, *Hasan al-Banna, al-da'iya al-imam wa-l-mujaddid al-shahid*. Damascus, Dar al-Qalam, 1421/2000
Mahmud, 'Ali 'Abd al-Halim, *Wasa'il al-tarbiya 'inda l-ikhwan al-muslimin*. Al-Mansura, Dar al-Wafa', 1989
al-Nafisi, 'Abdallah Fahd, ed., *al-Haraka al-islamiyya: ru'ya mustaqbaliyya. Awraq fi l-naqd al-dhati*. Cairo, Maktabat Madbuli, 1410/1989
al-Qaradawi, Yusuf, *al-Ikhwan al-muslimun. 70 'aman fi l-da'wa wa-l-tarbiya wa-l-jihad*. Cairo, Maktabat Wahba, 1999
Raslan, 'Uthman 'Abd al-Mu'izz, *al-Tarbiya al-islamiyya 'inda jama'at al-ikhwan al-muslimin, 1928–1954*. Cairo, Dar al-Tawzi' wa-l-Nashr al-Islamiyya, 1990
al-Imam al-shahid Hasan al-Banna bi-aqlam talamidhatihi wa-mu'asirih, ed. Jabir Rizq. Al-Mansura, Dar al-Wafa', 1406/1986
Shadi, Salah, *Safahat min al-tarikh. Hasad al-'umr*. Kuwait, Shirkat al-Shu'a' lil-Nashr, 1981
Sha'ir, Muhammad Fathi 'Ali, *Wasa'il al-i'lam al-matbu'a fi da'wat al-ikhwan al-muslimin*. Jidda, Dar al-Mujtama' lil-Nashr wa-l-Tawzi', 1405/1985
al-Sisi, 'Abbas, *Fi qafilat al-ikhwan al-muslimun*. Vol. 1, 2nd ed., Alexandria, Dar al-Tiba'a wa-l-Nashr wa-l-Sawtiyyat, 1987
al-Sisi, 'Abbas, *Hasan al-Banna. Mawaqif fi l-da'wa wa-l-tarbiya*. 2nd ed., Alexandria, Dar al-Da'wa, 1981 (1978)
Zaki, Muhammad Shawqi, *al-Ikhwan al-muslimun wa-l-mujtama' al-misri*. n.d., n.p. (1953)

SECONDARY LITERATURE

'Abd al-Baqi, 'Abir Hasan, *Tabaqat al-afandiyya fi misr fi l-nisf al-awwal min al-qarn al-'ishrin*. Cairo, Maktabat Madbuli, 2005

'Abd al-Jawwad, Muhammad, *Taqwim Dar al-'Ulum*. 2 vols., new ed., Cairo, Dar al-Hani lil-Tiba'a wa-l-Nashr, 1411/1991

Abdalla, Ahmed, *The Student Movement and National Politics in Egypt 1923–1973*. London, Al Saqi Books, 1985

Ammann, Ludwig, "Kommentiertes Literaturverzeichnis zu Zeitvorstellungen und geschichtlichem Denken in der islamischen Welt," *Die Welt des Islams*, 37, 1997, pp. 28–87

Armbrust, Walter, *Mass Culture and Modernism in Egypt*. Cambridge, Cambridge University Press, 1996

Aroian, Lois A., *The Nationalization of Arabic and Islamic Education in Egypt: Dar-al-'Ulum and Al-Azhar*. Cairo, American University in Cairo Press, 1983 (Cairo Papers in Social Science 6, 4)

Badran, Margot, *Feminists, Islam, and Nation: Gender and the Making of Modern Egypt*. Princeton, Princeton University Press, 1995

al-Banna, Jamal, *al-Sayyid Rashid Rida, munshi' al-Manar wa-ra'id al-salafiyya al-haditha*. Cairo, Dar al-Fikr al-Islami, 2006

Baraka, Magda, *The Egyptian Upper Class between Revolutions 1919–1952*. Reading, Ithaca, 1998

Baron, Beth, *Egypt as a Woman: Nationalism, Gender, and Politics*. Berkeley, Los Angeles, University of California Press, 2005

——, *The Women's Awakening in Egypt: Culture, Society, and the Press*. New Haven, London, Yale University Press, 1994

Beinin, Joel and Zachary Lockman, *Workers on the Nile: Nationalism, Communism, Islam, and the Egyptian Working Class, 1882–1954*. Princeton, Princeton University Press, 1987

al-Bishri, Tariq, *al-Haraka al-islamiyya fi misr 1945/1957 (muraja'a wa-taqdim jadid)*. 2nd ed., Cairo, Dar al-Shuruq, 1983 (1972)

Bonner, Michael, *Jihad in Islamic History: Doctrines and Practice*. Princeton, Oxford, Princeton University Press, 2006

Brown, Nathan J., *Peasant Politics in Modern Egypt: The Struggle Against the State*. New Haven, London, Yale University Press, 1990

Carter, Barbara L., "On Spreading the Gospel to Egyptians Sitting in Darkness: The Political Problem of Missionaries in Egypt in the 1930s," *Middle Eastern Studies*, 20, 1984, pp. 18–36

Chih, Rachida, *Le Soufisme au quotidien. Confréries d'Egypte au XXe siècle*. Paris, Sindbad, 2000

Cook, David, *Martyrdom in Islam*. Cambridge, Cambridge University Press, 2007

——, *Understanding Jihad*. Berkeley, Los Angeles, University of California Press, 2005

Costet-Tardieu, Francine, *Un réformiste à l'université al-Azhar: Oeuvre et pensée de Mustafa al-Maraghi (1881–1945)*. Cairo, Paris, CEDEJ and Karthala, 2005

Cromer, The Earl of, *Modern Egypt*, new ed., London, Macmillan, 1911 (1908)

Danielson, Virginia, *The Voice of Egypt: Umm Kulthum, Arabic Song, and Egyptian Society in the Twentieth Century*. Chicago, London, University of Chicago Press, 1997

Dawud, Muhammad 'Abd al-'Aziz, *al-Jam'iyyat al-islamiyya fi misr wa-dawruha fi nashr al-da'wa al-islamiyya*. Cairo, al-Zahra' lil-I'lam al-Arabi, 1992

Deeb, Marius, *Party Politics in Egypt: the Wafd & its Rivals 1919–1939*. London, Ithaca Press, 1979

De Jong, Fred, *Turuq and Turuq-Linked Institutions in Nineteenth-Century Egypt*. Leiden, Brill, 1978

Douglas, J. Leigh, *The Free Yemeni Movement 1935–1962*. Beirut, The American University of Beirut, 1987

Eccel, A. Chris, *Egypt, Islam and Social Change: Al-Azhar in Conflict and Cooperation*. Berlin, Klaus Schwarz Verlag, 1994

El-Shohoumi, Nadia, *Der Tod im Leben. Eine vergleichende Analyse altägyptischer und rezenter ägyptischer Totenbräuche. Eine phänomenologische Studie*. Vienna, Verlag der Österreichischen Akademie der Wissenschaften, 2004

Ende, Werner, *Arabische Nation und islamische Geschichte. Die Umayyaden im Urteil arabischer Autoren des 20. Jahrhunderts*. Wiesbaden, Franz Steiner, 1977

Farag, Iman, "Éduquer les éducateurs: les revues pédagogiques égyptiennes de l'entre-deux-guerres," *Revue des mondes musulmans et de la Méditerranée*, 95–98, 2002, pp. 336–54

Fortna, Benjamin C., "Islamic Morality in Late Ottoman 'Secular' Schools," *International Journal of Middle East Studies*, 32, 2000, pp. 369–93

——, *Imperial Classroom: Islam, the State, and Education in the Late Ottoman Empire*. Oxford, Oxford University Press, 2002

Gaffney, Patrick Daniel, "The Office of 'Al-Wa'iz' and the Revival of Preaching in Egypt," *Mélanges de l'Institut Dominicain d'Études Orientales*, 17, 1986, pp. 247–56

Gallagher, Nancy E., *Egypt's Other Wars: Epidemics and the Politics of Public Health*. Syracuse, NY, Syracuse University Press, 1990

Gershoni, Israel, "The Muslim Brothers and the Arab Revolt in Palestine," *Middle Eastern Studies*, 22, 1986, pp. 367–97

——, and James P. Jankowski, *Egypt, Islam, and the Arabs: the Search for Egyptian Nationhood, 1900–1930*. New York, Oxford, Oxford University Press, 1986

——, and James P. Jankowski, *Redefining the Egyptian Nation, 1930–1945*. Cambridge, Cambridge University Press, 1995

Glaß, Dagmar, *Der Muqtataf und seine Öffentlichkeit: Aufklärung, Räsonnement und Meinungsstreit in der frühen arabischen Zeitschriftenkommunikation*. 2 vols., Würzburg, Ergon, 2004

Haydar, Khalil 'Ali, *Adwa' 'ala mudhakkirat Hasan al-Banna*. Kuwait, Shirkat Kazima, 1989

Haykal, Muhammad Husayn, *Mudhakkirat fi l-siyasa al-misriyya*. 3 vols., Cairo, Dar al-Ma'arif, 1977, 1978

Heyworth-Dunne, James, *An Introduction to the History of Education in Modern Egypt*. London, Luzac, 1939

Hoffman, Valerie J., *Sufism, Mystics, and Saints in Modern Egypt*. Columbia, SC, University of South Carolina Press, 1995

Imady, Omar, *Journals, Associations and Political Parties: the Institutions of Islamic Reform (1871–1949)*. Unpublished doctoral thesis, University of Pennsylvania, 1993

Jankowski, James P., *Egypt's Young Rebels: "Young Egypt," 1933–1952*. Stanford, Stanford University Press, 1975

Kinsey, David C., "Efforts for Educational Synthesis under Colonial Rule: Egypt and Tunisia," *Comparative Educational Review*, 15, 1971, 2, pp. 172–87

Knysh, Alexander, *Islamic Mysticism: A Short History*. Leiden, Brill, 2000

Krämer, Gudrun, "Aus Erfahrung lernen? Die islamische Bewegung in Ägypten," in *Religiöser Fundamentalismus: Vom Kolonialismus zur Globalisierung*, ed. Clemens Six, Martin Riesebrodt and Siegfried Haas. Innsbruck, Studien Verlag, 2004, pp. 185–200

——, *Gottes Staat als Republik: Reflexionen zeitgenössischer Muslime zu Islam, Menschenrechten und Demokratie*. Baden-Baden, Nomos, 1999

——, *The Jews in Modern Egypt 1914–1952*. Seattle, University of Washington Press, 1989

——, "Justice in Modern Islamic Thought," in *Shari'a: Islamic Law in the Contemporary Context*, ed. Abbas Amanat and Frank Griffel. Stanford, Stanford University Press, 2007, pp. 20–37

Kramer, Martin, *Islam Assembled: The Advent of the Muslim Congresses*. New York, Columbia University Press, 1986

Kühn, Peter, "Bildung und Erziehung im Konzept der ägyptischen Muslimbruderschaft unter Hasan al-Banna," *Orient*, 33, 1992, 2, pp. 253–64

Kugle, Scott, *Rebel Between Spirit and Law: Ahmad Zarruq, Sainthood, and Authority in Islam*. Bloomington and Indianapolis, Indiana University Press, 2006

al-Kumi, Sami 'Abd al-'Aziz, *al-Sihafa al-islamiyya fi misr fi l-qarn al-tasi''ashar*. Al-Mansura, Dar al-Wafa', 1992

Kupferschmidt, Uri, "The Muslim Brothers and the Egyptian Village," *Asian and African Studies*, 16, 1982, pp. 157–70

Lia, Brynjar, *The Society of the Muslim Brothers in Egypt: the Rise of an Islamic Mass Movement 1928–1942*. Reading, Ithaca, 1998

Lübben, Ivesa, "'Die Träume von heute sind die Wahrheiten von morgen ...' – Geschichtsbewusstsein und Zeitkonzeptionen bei Hasan al-Banna," in *Religion, Staat und Politik im Vorderen Orient. Festschrift für Friedemann Büttner*, ed. Amr Hamzawy and Ferhad Ibrahim, Münster, Hamburg, London, LIT, 2003, pp. 233–62

Makarius, Raoul, *La Jeunesse intellectuelle d'Égypte au lendemain de la deuxième guerre mondiale*. The Hague, Mouton, 1960

Marlow, Louise, *Hierarchy and Egalitarianism in Islamic Thought*. Cambridge, Cambridge University Press, 1997

Mayeur-Jaouen, Catherine, "Les débuts d'une revue néo-salafiste: Muhibb al-Din al-Khatib et Al-Fath de 1926 à 1928," *Revue des mondes musulmans et de la Méditerranée*, 56–58, 2002, pp. 227–55

——, *Pèlerinages d'Égypte. Histoire de la piété copte et musulmane XVe-XXe siècles*. Paris, Éditions de l'École des Hautes Études en Sciences Sociales, 2005

Meijer, Roel, *The Quest for Modernity: Secular Liberal and Left-Wing Political Thought in Egypt, 1945–1958*. Amsterdam, Amsterdam University, 1995

Mitchell, Richard P., *The Society of the Muslim Brothers*, new ed., New York, Oxford, Oxford University Press, 1993

Mitchell, Timothy, *Colonising Egypt*. Cambridge, Cambridge University Press, 1988

Murre-van den Berg, Helen, ed., *New Faiths in Ancient Lands: Western Missions in the Middle East in the Nineteenth and Early Twentieth Centuries*. Leiden, Brill, 2006

Na'im, Khalid Muhammad, *al-Judhur al-tarikhiyya li-irsaliyyat al-tansir al-ajnabiyya fi misr (1756–1986). Dirasa watha'iqiyya*. Cairo, Kitab al-Mukhtar, 1988

Nieuwkerk, Karin van, *"A Trade like Any Other." Female Singers and Dancers in Egypt*. Austin, University of Texas Press, 1995

Padwick, Constance E., *Muslim Devotions: A Study of Prayer-Manuals in Common Use*. London, Oneworld, 1961, 1996

al-Qaradawi, Yusuf, a*l-Waqt fi hayat al-muslim*. 5th ed., Cairo, Maktabat Wahba, 2007

Qutb, Sayyid, *A Child from the Village*. Cairo, American University Press, 2005

Ramadan, Tariq, *Aux sources du renouveau musulman*. Lyon, Éditions Tawhid, 2002

Reid, Donald Malcolm, *Cairo University and the Making of Modern Egypt*. Cambridge, Cambridge University Press, 1990

Rizq, Qustandi, *al-Musiqa al-sharqiyya wa-l-ghina' al-'arabi*. 2nd ed., Cairo, Maktabat Madbuli, 2000

Ryzova, Lucie, *L'effendiyya ou la modernité contestée*. Cairo, CEDEJ, 2004

Salim, Jamal, *al-Bulis al-misri yahkum misr, 1910–1952*. Cairo, al-Thaqafa al-'Arabiyya, n.d.

Sharkey, Heather J., *American Evangelicals in Egypt: Missionary Encounters in an Age of Empire*. Princeton, Oxford, Princeton University Press, 2008

Smiles, Samuel, *Self-Help: With Illustrations of Character, Conduct, and Perseverance*, ed. Peter W. Sinnema. Oxford, Oxford University Press, 2002 (London 1859; rev. 2nd ed., 1866)

Smith, Charles D., "The 'Crisis of Orientation': the Shift of Egyptian Intellectuals to Islamic Subjects in the 1930s", *International Journal of Middle East Studies*, 4, 1973, pp. 382–440

Smith, Wilfred Cantwell, *Islam in Modern History*. Princeton, Princeton University Press, 1957

Starrett, Gregory, *Putting Islam to Work: Education, Politics, and Religious Transformation in Egypt*. Berkeley, University of California Press, 1998

Steppat, Fritz, *Tradition und Säkularismus im modernen ägyptischen Schulwesen bis zum Jahre 1952*. Unpublished Habilitation thesis, Freie Universität Berlin, 1964

Talima, 'Isam, *Hasan al-Banna wa-tajribat al-fann*. Cairo, Maktabat Wahba, 1429/2008

Yusuf, al-Sayyid, *al-Ikhwan al-muslimun*. 3 vols., Cairo, Markaz al-Mahrusa, 1994

INDEX